THE
WEDGE

*How to Stop Selling
and Start Winning*

**The Only Proven Technique for Separating Prospective Clients From
Your Competitors and Winning New Business**

www.thewedge.net

RANDY SCHWANTZ

▼

The National Underwriter Company
5081 Olympic Blvd.
Erlanger, KY 41018

International Standard Book Number: 0-87218-371-8

Printed in the United States of America

Dedication

I want to dedicate this book to my mom and dad. When I turned eight years old, my dad started taking me on road trips. We would call on five or ten of his customers and get orders. He taught me to respect and love the profession of selling.

And my mom told me a million times, "there's nothing you can't do if you just make up your mind that's what you want to do." Great advice, mom!

Thanks mom and dad for your leadership, direction and encouragement. I love you.

Acknowledgement

Thank you Michael Graham, I could have never written this book without your help; Kevin Grant for encouraging me to develop "The Wedge"; and Pat Bonds for encouraging me to focus on this industry. And Mary Jo, thanks for your loyalty and persistence in helping develop the program that this book is based on.

I want to thank my clients for your willingness to learn and for accommodating my endless questioning of your conversations, strategies and techniques in an effort to find a better way to sell

And to my wife and kids, thanks for giving me the freedom to focus on this project on nights and weekends when we should have been outside playing or I should have been giving baths.

Thank you all.

Contents

Preface

The Mission

Are you on a mission?

Corporations have a mission statement plus long and short-term financial goals. At what stage in a producer's career does he identify and quantify his own personal financial goals, his own mission?

Ten years ago, this guy ruined my life.

I was doing a sales training session in Houston. It was one of those late summer days in Texas when the skies open up and a deluge floods the city. We were beyond introductions and starting into the meat of the workshop when a latecomer entered the room. He was dripping wet, bleary-eyed and exhausted. He looked too miserable to ignore.

Me: *"Join us. You look like you've had a tough night."*

Salesperson: *"Sorry. My daughter just started college. I drove her there yesterday, got her all set up, then back home overnight, an eleven hour drive. Sorry I'm late."*

Me: *"Tough drive in this rain."*

Salesperson: *"You can say that again."*

Me: *"Where's your daughter going to school?"*

Salesperson: *"Texas Tech."*

Me: *"Did you put her in an apartment or a dorm?"*

Salesperson: *"An apartment."*

Me: *"What floor?"*

Salesperson: *"Third floor."*

Me: *"You have any help carrying everything up or just yourself?"*

Salesperson: *"Just me."*

Me: *"No wonder you're tired. I bet your back hurts too. Do you have other kids in school?"*

Salesperson: *"Yes, this is my second."*

Me: *"Where is she?"*

Salesperson: *"She's at Texas Tech also."*

Me: *"At least the good news is that it's all paid for isn't it?"*

Salesperson: *The salesperson dropped his head, shook it back and forth while saying, "No, it isn't."*

I was thinking, oh my gosh. Didn't he know eighteen years ago, when this kid was born that she'd be going off to school? Why didn't he prepare for it? He's a Risk Manager. He's all about preparation. Why didn't he do it for himself? In fact, this guy had a large book of business and made very good money. How did he let himself get into this financial stress?

Then I started thinking.

Here I was, father of three daughters and one on the way. I was making a comfortable living and slowly growing my income. At the end of every year I tucked a few dollars into an education account for the girls and my own IRA. It was what I thought I could afford, but I didn't know if it was enough.

So I sat down with an investment advisor and told him the story about the guy in Houston and said "I don't want to be like him ten to fifteen years from now. I've got four daughters. I already know I need to buy four cars, four university tuitions, four weddings, and also fund my own retirement. I want to know, how much money do I need to save every year to accomplish that?"

He got his pencil, calculator, and a sheet of paper. About five minutes later he said, "Are you ready?" I'm thinking to myself, is it that bad? He then told me, "In order for you to do the things you told me you wanted to do — the cars, universities, weddings and retirement, you have to save about $65,000 a year after tax." I'm thinking no way. At that point in my life, after making a house payment, utilities and paying for taxes, cars, private school tuition, and all the other stuff we had going on, I was able to save about $6,000 a year. Now I've got to save ten times that much?

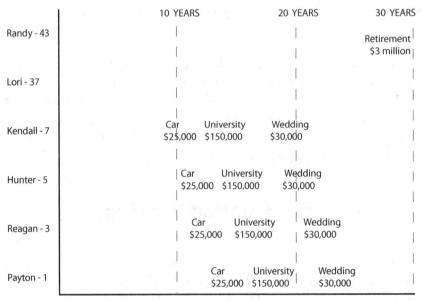

THIRTY YEAR TIMELINE

To fund all these obligations Randy must save $65,000 annually. Ouch!

I needed to radically increase my personal income. . . soon.

Like most people, I had monthly and annual sales goals. And, I would love to tell you that I was deeply inspired to achieve them, but that wouldn't really be the truth. Most of the goal setting I had done up to that point was just that, throw a challenge goal out there, aim for the stars, and who knows maybe I'd hit one. But, they were just numbers and it didn't feel real. Things really changed when I made a list with my daughters and wife, along with their current ages. I then plotted out on a timeline when I would need money for Kendall's car, her university tuition, and a wedding. And then I did it again for Hunter, and again for Reagan, and again for Payton, four times, once for each girl. Then I started thinking about Lori and me. I put us on the timeline with our current ages and projected when I wanted to retire and how much money I wanted to have in the bank at that point in the future. It wasn't until then that it became very real and I became very motivated, a man on a mission.

That guy in Houston ruined my life, making me think about all this stuff. I was miserable for awhile, totally overwhelmed with the truth about my responsibility. Consider this: the average household income in America in 2007 was $50,233. All I had to do was increase my personal income by over twice what the average family earns so I could pay Uncle Sam about $35,000 and keep $65,000 to prefund my future.

But now, rather than having random goals of do better, make more, be a high achiever, I had a goal that was personal. It wasn't just about me, it was about my family. It was about putting myself in a position to say "yes" to them. The good news is I had time. If I had waited, I'm sure we would have gotten by somehow, everyone does. But, I didn't want to be one of those guys that just gets by. I wanted to be a high achiever for a very real and tangible reason. I have four beautiful daughters and a great wife and I wanted to provide for them.

By the way, that's a real story. It began about ten years ago when Kendall was 7, Hunter 5, Reagan 3, and Payton had just been born. I think about it every day; it inspires me. My family and I have been blessed by people like you who buy my books, take my training, and introduce me into your agencies and businesses. As I result, I can tell you that in ten years, I not only achieved what I set out to do but was able to double it. I believe you can too when you get really clear about what's important and commit to it.

Here's a question for you. What's your inspiration? What makes you want to give it your all every day? I've polled almost 3,000 producers and sales people with a couple of simple questions. What's your new business and growth goal for the year? How did you come up with it? Was it assigned to you by a sales manager or is it really yours? Did you just kind of pick it out of the air? Or, have you done some very serious thinking, mapping, and strategizing on exactly how much money you need to make every year to not only pay your bills, take a vacation, and own a nice home but to also make serious progress toward funding your family's future.

I find it interesting that out of the 3,000 producers I've polled, 10 percent or less had a plan that was longer than twelve months. And, in many cases, the plan or twelve-month goal was more an obligation to the sales manager or agency principal than a commitment to themselves and their family.

My speaking coach, Robin Robins, said that everyone has a strategy for deciding where they will invest their money.

1. Plan carefully. They budget what they are going to spend, making investments in what is going up in value.
2. Spend everything they make. They may invest small amounts of money, but they mostly buy cars, toys, vacations, etc.
3. Spend every penny they can get their hands on plus whatever they can borrow. They have a negative net worth.

Her insight was clear and simple. The first group is wealthy. The second group is largest, classified as middle class, getting nowhere financially, and retiring dependent on social security and a modest IRA or 401k. The last group is essentially bankrupt, having spent their money on things they couldn't afford.

An empty bank account is the result of a lifetime of poor decisions.

Napoleon Hill said millionaires and the wealthy have special-ized knowledge. The wealthy invest in things that go up in value. What is the one thing you have spent money on that has consis-tently gone up in value? I trust it's going to be YOU!

Successful producers don't just happen. They have personal goals that are enormously important, and they use their business as a means to achieve them. They are investors in the market and in their businesses, but mostly in themselves.

iWin

Throughout this book, the mantra is "stop selling and start winning." But what does winning really mean? One way to define Winning is:

Increasing your

- **Wealth**

- **Income**

- **Net worth**

Remember when you were a kid, playing a pick up basketball game or the latest video game with your friends? You were dying to fire that last shot because you wanted to be the one that shouted, "I win!" Fast forward to today. Picture yourself coming up on the eighteenth hole with a close score. You count up the strokes and say with a big ole smile, I win.

Winning is fun. But it's also meaningful, particularly in the context of "iWin." Because to me it simply means Increasing your Wealth, Income, and Net worth — iWin.

Your **wealth** is basically your liquidity—those dollars under your direct access and control. Your **income** is your current salary, bonuses, and commissions, plus that of your partner. Your **net worth** is tougher. You may have money in your pocket, a beautiful home, a fast car, and a killer collection of rare medieval manuscripts, but how much of that is already leveraged with debt? Your net worth is simply what you have minus what you owe. And for most Americans the spread between those numbers is not very wide. In the game of personal finance, if you want to be able to say I win, all those measure have to grow, particularly the later.

From Here to iWin (Increasing Wealth, Income, and Net Worth)

I met Austen almost ten years ago. He had about a $300,000 book of business, managing nearly 300 accounts. He spent the majority of his life renewing what he had. Today he handles thirty accounts valued at $1,300,000. Pretty big transformation in ten years. How did he do it? He drew out his timeline with a focus on his children and wife and set his goals. Inspired to make a difference for his family as well as his prospects, he made a few sacrifices. The first sacrifice was to give up a whole bunch of small accounts that kept him busy but didn't make him any money. With his time freed up, he perfected The Wedge — some of which you will learn in this book. He picked his prospects carefully, targeting them with a very compelling message as he made cold calls. He set his appointments, Wedged the incumbent, and won the business. Then he had the audacity to ask his client to introduce him into their relationships. He'd go to prospects on a red carpet introduction, wedge those guys, and win again. Like a Maytag washing machine, he just kept repeating that cycle.

In my opinion, he had two things going for himself. Sure he's a smart guy, but there are lots of smart guys and gals. Austen had the courage to make a simple commitment to himself. That's the biggest thing he had going. Secondly, he was in an agency with leaders committed to growth. As a result, they challenged him to do his best instead of applauding him because he was doing well.

What's going to be your biggest challenge to get to iWin? Number one is your ability to make a commitment. Secondly, your willingness to become a student — to study, learn, role play, and practice your craft. As a salesperson if you can treat your career as a sport instead of a profession, you'll practice, get really good, and have lots of fun playing. If you treat it like a profession, you might become too serious — take way too many technical courses, position yourself to impress the intellectuals, and get killed out on the playing field. Winning takes a balance of skills and talents. Sure, you have to have some degree of technical proficiency, but you absolutely must be a really great prospector and salesperson.

The other challenge is that if you do too well, you'll make a lot of people mad. Some of your colleagues will feel uncomfortable around you; some friends might get jealous. Many of your peers are vested in the belief that selling insurance is really hard and selling larger accounts is tougher still. Some sales people are so risk adverse that they're constantly afraid of losing their small accounts. They can't imagine how much it might hurt to lose a big one, so they play it safe and avoid that possibility entirely. I'm not telling you anything you don't already know, but winning a small account doesn't do much for the pocket book. It may make you feel better to have helped someone in need, but the needs of small, crappy clients can't be more important than the needs of your family. When you commit to your own and your family's future, you're going to leave some folks behind. And perhaps, a few will opt to follow your path. It happens.

Getting Organized

A young guy told me the other day he was great at setting goals, just lousy at following through. He asked me how often people should review them. I didn't know what to say except that I do it every Saturday morning. I pull up my Schwab account and write down how it did for the week. I go to my bank account and write down my balances. I go to my accounting software and write down sales and profitability. I've been doing it this way for years.

On the other hand, what I find really challenging as a consultant is when I go to an agency and ask about their Performance Indicators — like who sold how much in the past month, quarter, and year. What are their closing ratios? Any idea how many closed by Broker of Record Letter? After we get through with what many people call the lag indicators (how did you do in the past), I ask about the lead indicators. How much is in the pipeline? Can you tell me by producer? Can you tell me by month? Are the closing estimates even remarkably close to accurate? Can you easily break it down by specialty, i.e., manufacturing, construction, healthcare, or transportation?

Too often they say something like, let me call Sally in. In comes Sally. Hey Sally, could you get Mr. Schwantz some of the information he's asking for? Then I repeat everything again and wait for a couple weeks until she has time to get to it. At some point, my email goes ding. There's that email from Sally, right on time about three weeks after I asked for it. What a way to run a business! But the reality is this is how most, but not all, agencies operate. Their reporting of what's in the pipeline is difficult at best. And when they manage to pull it together, it's already a month out of date.

So, your next challenge is getting organized. Regardless of what your agency and sales manager do, you need a prospecting system that will help you keep up with your target prospects. I've seen a lot of systems. One very popular one is a yellow pad. The other is a business card stack. Or you could try Outlook. Thirty years ago, this was cutting edge stuff. It's just not anymore. So how are you going to organize your prospecting activity? There is one simple reason that this becomes extraordinarily relevant: if you don't, hundreds of thousands of dollars will fall through the cracks, slip through your fingers, end up in someone else's bank account. If you don't have iWin type goals, you won't care. If you've set real goals and become that man on a mission, it's pretty important to get a system going for yourself that is anchored in reality and works, an electronic net that captures your money.

Getting Really Good

If you play golf you know that almost every golfer has an opinion about what you should do to improve. Keep your left heel down, strengthen your grip, slow down your swing. You're standing too erect; you should be in an athletic position; keep your head still; turn your hips; don't turn your hips so much; lighten your grip. If you're not careful, you'll feel like a pretzel trying to play golf.

Like golf, opinions about selling are everywhere and no one knows it all. However, I'd make one little recommendation: find a system you like and a coach to go along with it and master that system. In your office and around your environment, I promise you'll find the "just get them to like you" relationship guy, the "save them money" price guy, the "find a coverage gap" coverage guy, and, if you're lucky, you'll find a few committed Wedge guys. If you're not careful your sales strategy will look like a pretzel and just might not be that effective.

Let me ask your opinion on this. If I wanted to really get better at golf, should I just buy one of Hank Haney's books on improving your golf game or would it be smart to go take a series of lessons from him? Do you really think he could teach something in person I couldn't learn out of his book?

iWin

If improving your wealth, income, and net worth is really your goal, then I've got one other little recommendation. But before I tell you what it is, let me tell you how it came about.

In the old days before technology entered out lives, sales people traveled with a trunk full of file boxes, leatherette folders crammed with business cards, a local Mapsco, and rolls of quarters for the pay phones. Seems like ancient history, because the world suddenly went wireless. Pretty soon we found ourselves carrying a cell phone, a GPS, an MP3 player, and a laptop so that we could stay in communication, didn't get lost, could listen to music, could check our email, and could check the daily stock report. We thought we were pretty cool… or maybe not. Along comes some Silicon Valley genius with the crazy idea of integrating all of this into one little handheld device. Practically overnight, it made all previous devices obsolete because they were cumbersome, required multiple battery chargers, and people needed a hunting vest or a backpack just to tote them around. The era of the smart phone began.

Well, I've been working on a little secret that will do for salespeople what smart phones have done for millions. It makes the life of a sales organization a lot easier. It starts by making your life better, then your sales manager's life better, then the CEO's life better. Maybe I've got that reversed, but you get my drift.

If you want some inside scoop go to iwin2.thewedge.net

Randy Schwantz
July 2010

Introduction
The Challenge:

Incumbent Agents Retain 92 percent of Their Accounts

When you target new commercial lines business you stand a good chance of winding up behind the eight ball. In all too many cases, a prospect will give you a chance to quote — and then use your quote to pressure the current (incumbent) agent into cutting his rate to keep the account. *That's why incumbent agents enjoy a 92 percent retention rate in commercial lines.* How can a producer break the relationship between her prospect and the incumbent agent and win? Keep reading!

A Typical Sales Call

Phase I

In this initial phase, the salesperson typically is not as prepared as he or she could be and probably has done little research. He goes in pretty cold.

Salesperson: *"Mr. Jones, tell me about your business."*

Prospect: *"We've been here for seven years. We make widgets."*

Salesperson: *"That's really interesting. Are you the owner?"*

Prospect: *"Yes, I am."*

1

Salesperson: *"That's great!" The reason I wanted to come by was to tell you about our agency and see if we could help you with any of your insurance problems."*

Prospect: *"Fine."*

Salesperson: *"We've been in business since 1942, we write lots of business like yours, we have great markets and we really take pride in providing great service. Is there anything wrong with your current program that you'd like me to fix?"*

Prospect: *"No, nothing that I can think of."*

Salesperson: *"Are you happy with your service?"*

Prospect: *"Yes, everything seems to be fine."*

Salesperson: *"Are you comfortable with the price you're paying?"*

Prospect: *"Oh it seems fair, but insurance is expensive."*

Salesperson: *"What I'd like to do is to get a copy of your policies and see if I can improve on your coverage. If I can do that, and save you money, is there any reason why you wouldn't be able to make a change?"*

Prospect: *"See what you can do and let's talk about it."*

Salesperson: *"Great! I just need copies of those policies and I'll get to work."*

The producer will take this information back to the office, fill out an application, send it off to the carrier, and wait to get a price back that can be put into a proposal. At the sales meeting next week, the sales manager or owner will ask the producer how the new business meeting went. More than likely the producer will tell the sales manager or owner that the prospect had no problems and just wanted a better price. Everyone in the sales meeting will then talk for a few minutes about the "fact" that all prospects are price buyers and that no one cares about service anymore.

Phase II

The producer will get the price from the carrier and is somewhat excited because it looks pretty cheap. He will then put it into a presentation package and call the prospect for a meeting. At the meeting:

Salesperson: *"Thanks for letting me come back out. I think we came up with something you're going to like."*

The salesperson then makes the presentation, shows the prospect how he found a gap in the coverage, how he closed it, and how he brought back a good price.

Prospect: *"You sure know your business. You've done a good job and we're certainly going to consider you. Let me review my other bids and we can talk in a few days."*

Salesperson: *"That sounds great. I'll call you on Friday."*

The producer then goes back to his office and the sales manager or owner asks him how the meeting went. The producer says "Great! I feel like we have a good chance. I've got a good relationship. I'll know Friday if I get it."

Phase III

Friday comes along and the producer is waiting by the telephone for the call that will reveal if he got the deal. The telephone never rings. At 3:00, the producer calls the prospect. The prospect is out. The producer then has a lousy weekend and spends it wondering if he got the deal. Monday comes along and the prospect finally returns the call. The following occurs:

Salesperson: *"I suppose you've made a decision. How did we do?"*

Prospect: *You were real competitive and did a very good job. I was impressed with your professionalism. Unfortunately the difference between your pricing* *and my current agent's just wasn't great enough to justify a move. I'd like you to stay in touch and work on it again next year. Thanks for your efforts."*

Salesperson: *Okay, I'll stay in touch and I look forward to working with you next year."*

The salesperson then makes the appropriate notes to call the prospect in nine months to ask the prospect again for the opportunity to bid.

At the next sales meeting, the sales manager or owner asks the producer how the opportunity turned out. The producer responds with "We got beat on price again. I think we should think hard about upgrading our marketing department, as well as the carriers we do business with. We've been beat on price a lot!"

Summary

Until this producer learns how to find the pain and get commitments, he will continue to get rolled. More importantly, his personal financial goals will continue to be put on hold. To WIN, he must learn how to Drive a Wedge between his prospect and the incumbent. If not, he will always believe that the problem is the marketing department and the carriers the agency represents.

The real problem is that this producer had a poor sales strategy. He could not find pain. He had a poor method for obtaining a clear agreement from the prospect not to let the incumbent agent have the last look and a chance to match his deal. Overall, he was not prepared.

This producer will probably not improve through normal experience or from attending typical agency sales meetings. He needs specialized training on how to find pain, break incumbent relationships, and eliminate last looks. The real problem he faces is that the incumbent has "the relationship," having worked with the client for at least one year, and in most cases, many years.

When a competing agent is asked, "What makes you better?" most agents will answer with, "We have a great reputation, great markets, have been in business a long time and offer great service!" When prospects hear this, their eyes roll back in their heads because they've heard this from almost everyone who walks through the door.

What most agents say make them better (great service, size, multiple markets or a strong reputation) is only the minimum acceptable standard for being in the game. These characteristics do not make an agency better; they make them the same as their competition.

This leads to the question — if the #1 problem is the incumbent and most agencies are really the same, then what does an agency have to sell other than price? Read on.

Chapter One

Stop Selling and Start Winning

"Winning isn't everything. It's the ONLY thing."

— Vince Lombardi

This book is the result of literally thousands of hours I have spent working with salespeople like you who were motivated, intelligent, productive…and frustrated. Frustrated because they were not achieving the high goals they had set for themselves.

What I have learned over the years has helped many of them achieve their personal goals of doubling or tripling their income, of having more time to invest in their families and personal relationships, and of achieving the professional success that eluded them for so long.

Like the salesperson outlined in the Challenge, they couldn't understand why they weren't successful more often, why deals that seemed all but certain one day frequently disappeared the next. What were they doing wrong?

Nothing. And everything.

Their mistake, the most common mistake made by businesspeople in America today, is their belief in "selling." Selling is important, but it is not the goal. Winning is the goal, and until you stop selling and start winning, you will never have the financial or personal success you desire.

"But Randy," a client asked me once, "How can I stop selling? I'm in sales….I'm a salesperson for cryin' out loud! What am I supposed to do?"

I'm not a motivational speaker or New Age guru. I'm not selling chicken soup for the salesman or the seven habits of the happy closer. I don't believe in magic formulas or psychic energy.

I'm a businessman and a sales coach. I believe in techniques, strategies, and sales tactics that have proven they work because they've been tested under fire, in the conference rooms and business suites of America. No stunts, no tricks, no gimmicks — just results.

Because I have spent so many years looking at the sales industry from a practical, bottom-line viewpoint, I've learned, in a very practical way, that the obstacle most salespeople must overcome to succeed is their dependency on "selling."

What Is Selling?

The simplest definition of selling I can give you is this: Every time you sit down with a prospect without a specific, well-developed, and effective strategy for winning, you are just selling. Period.

Selling is killing you out in the marketplace. It is wasting your time and your prospects. Anyone who says selling is hard is wrong. Selling is easy; winning is hard. Selling means making a good presentation. Winning means walking out with a check.

Selling is about looking good, prospecting, networking, "cocktailing," color-copying, binding, packaging, and e-mailing. Winning is about putting money in the bank.

In other words, selling is believing in the process, while winning is focusing on the results and crafting a specific, workable, well-rehearsed method to achieve those results.

What Is Your Focus?

The difference between selling and winning is focus. When you're selling, you're focused on yourself. You know everything there is to know about your product, your service, your company. But you know almost nothing about the prospect you are calling on.

Because you're so focused on yourself, you can probably think of a hundred reasons why everyone ought to hire you and fire your competition, but you probably can't come up with one specific reason why it would benefit the prospect sitting right in front of you. Instead of a specific strategy to close this deal by connecting with the prospect, your hope ("hope" is what you have left after you abandon hard work and planning) is that your product's benefits and features will somehow appeal to the prospect, and that she will make the connection for you.

As a result, your success depends completely on others. Even if you have the best deal, the best presentation, and the best personality, you are no closer to closing than the most amateur of your competitors. You're just counting on luck to get positive results for you.

What Is Your Intent?

Another key difference is *intent*. The intent of the "seller" is merely to stay in the game, to have a shot at quoting or making an offer. Sellers are focused on opportunities to pitch and present.

The winner is looking for opportunities to close. He enters *every* sales call with the intent to close, to walk out with a deal. Winners aren't playing numbers games, they aren't throwing their deals against a wall and hoping some will stick. They want every shot to count.

An example of this difference in intent is two skiers at the top of a mountain. One skier is focused on just making it down the hill and nothing more. He just wants to make it back to the lodge in one piece so he can come out another day and do it again. Whether he makes good time or not doesn't matter. He just wants to make it down one more time.

The other skier is focused on the course. He's looking at the turns, the curves, the trees, and the obstacles. He's not thinking about himself, he's focused on the course and how it needs to be skied. He begins the course with a plan specific to this course that will let him make the best possible time.

9

Which skier is going to finish first? Which skier is going to be the most successful? The one whose focus is not on himself and whose intent is to master the problem at hand.

How to Tell if You're "Selling"

As a sales coach who has worked with literally thousands of salespeople, I've noticed that many of them consider it a "win" just to get the chance to give a quote on a major account. They get estimates, they crunch numbers, package it up, run it through the color printer, put it in a glossy binder and hand it to their prospect, and then take a victory lap at their next sales meeting.

Back in the agency, the owner (or sales manager) and team members tell them "It's OK, don't worry if you don't get the account this time, maybe next year. It could take two to three years, just keep trying. It's all a numbers game."

The problem with that approach is that you'll starve to death before you make a living.

This is the epitome of selling: either the prospect will hear something he likes, or he won't. The salesperson's job is simply to get in front of as many prospects as possible and wait for lightning to strike.

What's Wrong with "Selling?"

Selling wastes a lot of time on unqualified prospects. When you're selling, you're going through the motions: making calls, looking for a chance to quote, playing the percentages. This makes salespeople, in essence, peddlers. A peddler is a guy that knows his product pretty well and goes out telling everyone they should use it. It's a numbers game. "If I call on enough people, I'll make a sale." It's a low percentage game however; too much time is wasted in the process of quoting non-buyers. Time that could have been used to sharpen skills, investigate further the real

10

needs of true prospects, and execute winning strategies to break incumbent relationships.

Selling allows the prospect to "use" you. When you go into a meeting with a prospect who has no intention of buying, you aren't just wasting your time, you're wasting his time, too. How does the prospect benefit from this meeting? By using you as an educational resource. You spend an hour telling him about potential gaps in his coverage, then, after you're gone, he calls the incumbent agent to talk over those ideas and see if they should be added to his current contract.

Selling keeps the focus on you and your efforts, not on the real problem. To sellers, sales is like Olympic ice skating; a solo sport in which the performer wins or loses based solely on her performance. If you prepare yourself well, have the right attitude, hit all the marks, and dazzle the crowd, you will score enough points to skate away with a gold medal contract and a bouquet of lucrative clients.

But sales isn't a solo sport. Sales is a contact sport. It's not figure skating — it's ice hockey. Sales is a sport in which, more often than not, someone else — the incumbent — is on the ice, controlling the puck.

And until you take the puck out of the incumbent's control and put it back in play, there is no opportunity to succeed. You can have a presentation with the production values of Pixar or James Cameron, paired with the positive attitude of Mohandas Ghandi, plus a price so low it would make a Republican blush, but as long as the incumbent is in control, the person you are meeting with is not a real prospect. He's just someone you are "selling" to.

The Two Problems Selling Can't Solve

The reason selling is so inefficient is that it is based on the faulty premise that there are two people in every sales call (you and the prospect) and that the most important person in the process is you, the salesperson. Nothing could be further from the truth.

11

There are, in fact, *three* people in every sales call — you, the prospect and the incumbent agent — and you are the *least* important person in the group. The other two people will determine whether or not you close the deal, and before you can close, you must solve two key problems.

Problem Number One: The Prospect Is Probably Lying

The number one problem facing people in sales is getting prospects to tell the truth. Overcome this problem, and you will become the most successful salesperson in America.

Why do prospects lie? Because they have no intention of buying. Their job is to check out their company's options, so they want to meet with you and get educated without actually buying from you. However, most people find hurting the feelings of others by rejecting their offer to be an unpleasant experience, so they tell you "little white lies" instead.

How do they do that? By giving you part of what you want — the opportunity to bid and for them to review your offer. In your meetings they nod politely as you spew out the familiar sales pitch of "quality service, competitive prices, and commitment to satisfaction." They compliment you on your professional presentation and maybe even let you buy them lunch, but when it's over, they pat you on your head and send you off to your next meeting.

Most of the prospects you call on have no interest in engaging in an honest dialogue with you, and you make it easy for them to avoid a dialogue by "selling" instead of listening. What could be easier for a prospect than answering a couple of simple, open-ended sales-school questions they've heard a hundred times before, then drinking a cup of coffee while you babble on with abstract statistics and rehearsed sales pitches? In most sales presentations, if the prospect did want to have an honest dialogue about what he and his firm wanted to accomplish, he would have to interrupt the seller to do it!

The businesspeople you call on don't want to have an honest, in-depth dialogue with you because they don't have any reason to believe that you are any different than every other salesperson. Honesty and dialogue involve effort and risk. Doing nothing is easy, and for your prospects, a little white lie such as "We'll get back to you later" goes a long way toward that end.

Problem Number 2:
The Incumbent Is Lying in Wait

The incumbent is the company and its agent who are currently providing the prospect the insurance products and services you offer. And, trust me, this incumbent has a direct, active role to play in any sales interview — whether or not she is actually sitting at the table.

Let's suppose that you are in a sales interview where you and the prospect immediately connect. Immediate rapport! She's speaking honestly to you about her company's needs and problems. She agrees that your company can provide the coverage needed. You get the information you need to come back with a proposal and when you do, your deal knocks her socks off. Is the deal done?

Not yet. Somebody has to deal with the third party in this triangle: the incumbent agent. And, because most people hate dispensing bad news and will do anything they can to avoid a confrontation, she isn't going to pick up the phone and tell her friendly, home-town agent to just "hit the road, Jack!"

No, she is going to tell her incumbent agent that she has received a very competitive proposal and her firm is thinking about making a change. When she does, her agent will come flying in the door before her phone even has a chance to cool off and ask for a last look. He will get it and then take your proposal back to his agency and return with an offer designed to get her to do the easiest thing in the world — nothing.

As the new agent, you are advocating change. Change is hard. The old, familiar agent—with essentially the same price and similar service — wants the prospect to do nothing. Doing nothing, not making a change, is the easiest way out for your prospect.

All of a sudden, instant rapport becomes immediate rejection. You've been "rolled," the incumbent got a last look and used the advantage of incumbency to block you out.

Getting "Rolled"

One of my sales trainees told the story of having an outstanding meeting with a new lead. The prospect was excited, impressed, and interested. He used phrases like "We will definitely look into this," and "Your price is outstanding, I am almost certain we can work together."

The agent left the meeting with the money practically jingling in his pocket, but when it came time to close...poof! The opportunity was gone. The prospect gave the agent the usual "We're looking at it closely, call me in a couple of weeks." Later, my trainee found out what really happened:

Not long after I walked out of his office, my prospect is on the phone with his incumbent agent, telling him *my* deal. The incumbent — my competitor — says something like "Yeah, that's a really good price...if you don't mind the back-end costs that are coming along."

My prospect gets nervous. "What kind of back-end costs?" His pal, the incumbent, is more than happy to tell him. "Well," he says, "it's kind of like the Yugo. Remember when that car first came out? Everyone saw the sticker price and was really impressed. The car looked good, had a nice paint job and a new body style and was incredibly cheap. Buyers soon discovered that it had high-maintenance costs and wasn't very dependable. That was a real problem."

After that, the deal had vaporized. It didn't matter how good my deal was, because the incumbent was there to kill it after I left. That's when I learned you've got to do more than just beat his price. You've got to eliminate the incumbent. If you don't, you'll get rolled.

My friend is right. You must have a strategy to deal with the incumbent, to reduce his credibility and the power of his solutions. Because if the prospect can't fire the incumbent, he isn't really a prospect. He's just wasting your time.

> *Be A Prophet! If you suspect your prospect is going to get a negative opinion about your product or service from a third party, bring it up. Tell him it is going to happen. It will take the sting out of it. Your prospect will be able to say "I knew you would say that!"*

The incumbent is always going to be there. He's never going to just disappear. You are trying to take money out of his pocket, and he's going to fight you to keep it. And in that fight, he's got the upper hand.

Was my friend really trying to sell the prospect an unreliable Yugo of a deal? No, but the prospect knew the incumbent. As a businessperson, he knew exactly how good (or bad) the service was that he was getting at the time. Change is difficult, it involves risk and effort. So, when the incumbent raised even the most unsubstantiated doubts about the new agent, the easiest thing in the world for the prospect to do was nothing. And if you're an incumbent, clients who do nothing are the best kind to have.

There's no question about it, the incumbent is going to try to roll you and to prevail you'll need a strategy to prevent it. In Chapter 11, you will learn a technique that is guaranteed to increase your chances of winning by 80 percent! You'll learn proven, tested strategies to overcome the incumbent agent's advantage, close the deal, and win.

So, What Do I Do Now?

Let's recap the real situation you face everyday as you try to "sell."

- In virtually every prospect meeting, there is an incumbent agent occupying your space.

- If the prospect can't fire the incumbent, she is not a prospect.
- The prospect does not want to speak honestly to you about his business.
- When you are "selling," you are learning nothing that can help you break the incumbent's relationship with the prospect.

Therefore, you have little chance of success.

Pretty clear problem, right? So what's the solution?

The solution is to stop selling and start winning. You can do this by developing a strategy that deals directly with each of these problems. You can learn how to drive a "wedge" between the prospect and the incumbent, to create space between the prospect and his incumbent agent. You can learn to use that space to beat the incumbent and close your deal.

I've developed a strategy that can do just that. It's called "The Wedge," and once you learn it, you will never have to "sell" again.

Chapter Two

The Two Problems
That Keep You "Selling"

Problem #1: The Incumbent

The single most important concept I have learned in my years as a sales coach and trainer is this: *Until you have a strategy to deal with the incumbent, you don't have a prospect.*

The incumbent is the person currently providing your prospect with the insurance products or services you sell. And, in almost every sales call you make or deal you pitch, the incumbent agent is a key player.

Why? Because of the laws of physics:

No Two Objects Can Occupy
the Same Space at the Same Time

Unless your agency has a niche that it has chosen to concentrate on, it's almost a certain bet that someone else sells insurance products or services similar to yours. And, unless you're calling on a brand-new business, chances are there is someone providing your services to the prospects you call on. That provider — your competition — is the incumbent agent.

The incumbent is occupying the space you need, and as long as he is there, you cannot close your deal. Prospects — business owners, CFOs, risk managers and the like — are always willing to

17

meet with you, of course. A meeting with you is a great way to get a briefing on new products or services available in the marketplace. This information is certainly worth an hour of their time and the price of a cup of coffee.

However, you can be confident of one thing: Before the prospect ever makes a change, he is going to go to his incumbent — the person currently occupying your space — and give him a last look at whatever deal you put together. After all, the incumbent is the current service provider. He has a standing relationship with the prospect. It is the most natural thing in the world, therefore, for him to be given a chance to match your offer.

Unless you have a strategy to deal with that fact, the incumbent will put together a deal that keeps the prospect from making a change. The incumbent will talk to his good friend, put together a good enough deal to keep the prospect from making a change (who likes change anyway?) and cut you out.

Congratulations, you've just been rolled. All of your work, all of your leads, all of your time has been wasted. Why? Because you never had a prospect to start with, you just had someone to sell to.

An Object at Rest Tends to Stay at Rest

By definition, when you are pitching a prospect, you are asking him to make a change. Change is difficult and consumes precious time and energy. It is always easier to do nothing... which is exactly what the incumbent wants.

No matter how well known your agency is, no matter what its reputation, when you ask a prospect to end a long-standing relationship with the incumbent, you are asking him to take a chance. Your agency may have been around for fifty years, but not for the prospect.

The person who has been there for the prospect is that familiar face, the guy who brings a gift basket by every Thanksgiving, his good friend, the incumbent. And you want him to break up that relationship.

So, when you present a deal that saves the prospect 20 percent he may be tempted to jump on it. But in fact, the best solution for him (from an inertia standpoint) would be to have the same deal provided by his friendly old incumbent. So what does the prospect do? He calls the incumbent, of course!

The incumbent will stop by, sit across the desk as he has done so many times before, and remind the prospect how good things are right now.

"Now, Joe," the incumbent will say, "we've known each other for ten years. I know our price isn't the lowest, but we've always been there for you. You know that you can pick up the phone and call me and I'll be there…a friendly, familiar face. Why, we even bought a table at your favorite charity fund-raiser last year. Me and the missus sat right across from you, remember?"

So, before you go and do anything rash, let me talk to my people and see what we can do. I can't promise we'll match that price, but we'll make it easy for you to keep doing what you're doing."

And, unless you have a strategy to deal with it, that's exactly what Joe the Prospect will do. The incumbent will put together a deal that is "good enough." It will be close enough to yours to allow the prospect to justify doing what he *wants* to do…nothing.

The prospect's desire to do nothing is a force of nature that gives the incumbent agent an advantage over you in every deal — even if the agent is lousy. That's why you need a plan to overcome that advantage before you even sit down with the prospect.

For Every Action, There Is an Equal and Opposite Reaction

For too many producers, the solution to the incumbent agent is to *push*. Pushing is a classic symptom of selling.

By pushing, I mean going on the attack, demeaning the incumbent, demonstrating why you would have to be an idiot to keep that agency over your own. The prospect, who has in fact done just that, will get your message loud and clear. And if you want someone to become defensive and dishonest, talk negatively about the choices they've made.

It's been said by millions of professionals that it is unprofessional to trash your competition. Perhaps that's so, but is that the real reason most people don't do it? Probably not. The real reason is that it doesn't work.

Why? Because nobody wants to be told they're stupid and if I'm the prospect and I hired the current agent and you tell me what a lousy decision that was, you're not attacking the incumbent — you're demeaning my ability to make decisions. I'm sitting behind my desk and you walk in, insinuate that I'd made bad decisions and then ask me to do you a favor and buy from you? You've got to be kidding.

That's why it's a mistake to jump on the prospect's first indication of dissatisfaction, like a shark attacking a wounded swimmer. While your goal is to drive a wedge between the prospect and the incumbent agent, if you attack, the prospect will feel like you are making *him* look bad for making the wrong choice. The harder you attack (your action), the more defensive the prospect will become (his equal and opposite reaction).

Once again, this is simple human nature. People don't like to acknowledge their mistakes, and making that mistake more obvious doesn't make them feel any better about it. Therefore, your difficult task is to help the prospect reveal his dissatisfaction with his incumbent agent, but without making him feel defensive. You want the prospect to ask you to help him make a change, not get into an argument about whether or not he needs to make one. That is why you need an incumbent strategy for every prospect.

Never attack your competitors. Let the prospect do it!

Problem #2: Honest, Open Dialogue

The other major problem that keeps you selling instead of winning is the unwillingness of the prospect to tell you the truth. This unwillingness is what keeps your incompetent (incumbent) competitors alive, and you dead on arrival.

Let's return to the laws of physics. Here is the situation:

1. The incumbent is occupying your space.

2. Inertia is keeping him there.

3. If you start pushing the prospect by attacking the incumbent, the prospect is likely to perceive it as an attack against him and start pushing back.

What you need to overcome these conditions is what Sir Isaac Newton would have called "an outside force."

That outside force is the prospect's own dissatisfaction with the incumbent. That dissatisfaction may be clearly evident to the prospect before you even show up, or it may be buried in the back of his mind. It could simply be that the prospect thinks his incumbent agent is doing a good job because he has no idea that it can be done better.

Whatever the source, if there is dissatisfaction, frustration, disappointment or concern (I use the term "pain" to describe all of these), that "pain" can be used to drive a wedge between the prospect and the incumbent. The emotional power of this pain is the outside force that can overcome the incumbent's position and move him out of the picture.

Pain is absolutely essential to your success if you want to break apart incumbent relationships and close deals. But to find it, you need an honest, open rapport with the prospect.

Don't *Nail* Your Prospects

The challenge you face during the sales call is to create an environment in which the prospect *wants* to tell you the truth. Without this environment, you are stuck selling, pitching features and benefits that may or may not provide solutions and counting on the prospect to figure that out. It doesn't matter how good your pitch is, either. If you can't make the emotional connection with your prospect, you won't find pain and you won't close deals. Here's an example.

I was talking to a prospect from Tennessee and, as a professional salesperson who knows my product and its value to my prospects, I became overzealous. I wanted to really nail him to the wall, and I hit him too hard and too fast with a couple of Wedges that revealed too plainly that he clearly needed my services. However, I had not taken enough time to develop an honest relationship with him, one built on trust and an open dialogue.

When I finished nailing him with my Wedges, I had put him in a position where he would have to be an idiot not to hire me. However, at an emotional level he didn't *want* to hire me. Not wanting to be an idiot, either, he became very uncomfortable and found a way to end the meeting without making any commitments.

Instead of using The Wedge as a tool for discovery, I had used it as a weapon. I was attempting to bludgeon the prospect into submission using my superior sales techniques, rather than helping him discover for himself the problems he had that he would like to solve and how I might be able to help solve them.

People Always Find a Way to Do What They Really Want to Do

This is a *key* point: People will find a way to justify doing what they want to do. And in most cases, what most people want to do is "nothing." Through the sellers I have coached, I've seen hundreds of situations where the salesperson brought in a deal that was clearly better than the incumbent's, but the prospect refused to make a change... simply because they didn't want to. The best deal didn't get it done. Once again, the incumbent held the trump card.

How can you get the prospect to want to make the change? An essential step is to make contact, to create a level of rapport that allows the prospect to tell you what she is really trying to accomplish and what her true needs are. When the prospect is comfortable with you and is confident that you can help her accomplish her goals, she will want to work with you, and the dynamics will begin to change. Remember, if the prospect wants to work with you, she will find a way to do so.

A Sympathetic Ear

One way to look at The Wedge is as a way to use emotional energy to overcome the incumbent's advantage. However, this depends heavily on the prospect's willingness to explore his own emotions, to talk honestly about what he wants to accomplish, and to feel comfortable sharing some of that information with you.

The wrong approach is to sell, to demonstrate how much you know about you, to ignore what the prospect has to say about himself, and to do everything possible to sound just like everyone else. Lecturing the prospect and attacking the incumbent are techniques that are commonly used in sales, but they don't help the prospect on his path of self-discovery.

Instead, I suggest you use the power of sympathetic listening.

Ever notice the interrogation style of the detectives in those television crime dramas? Gone are the physical threats and bare light bulbs. Intimidation seldom works. And if the frustrated police interrogator tries it, the suspect immediately screams for a lawyer.

Most of the time, the detective's first strategy is to win the suspect's trust. He makes him comfortable with a cold drink or cigarette (also good for surreptitiously collecting DNA samples). He demonstrates compassion and empathy for the situation in which the suspect finds himself. He might relate a story of his own frustration or that of a friend in a tricky situation. He suggests to the suspect that whatever happened, it probably wasn't the way it appears on the surface. It was an accident. Or the crime was committed by someone else entirely. And the best thing that the suspect can do in order to straighten things out and help himself is to tell his story, his way. The suspect is encouraged to talk about his betrayal, his anger, his desire to make things right. The most successful fictional (and real-life) detectives are part psychiatrist/part best friend/part spiritual confessor.

Contemporary detectives are not trying to obtain a confession to the crime during the first interrogation. They are taking the suspect's emotional temperature, identifying his triggers and his motives. They want to know what makes him tick and what gets him ticked off. They want to know if he trusts anyone or doesn't. They want to get his measure as a human being. Detectives also pretend to be riveted by his story, asking for elaboration on fine points and minutiae. Where was he at the time? Who was with him? All the while, they are making careful note of these details. As additional information from forensics and eye-witnesses is uncovered, any lies the suspect told during that initial interrogation become a noose around his neck. The detective simply has to give him enough rope.

Childlike Curiosity

My daughter Kendall finds things out the same way. She will often walk up to me and ask me a question and when she does, she'll kind of tilt her head and get this look on her face that says "I'm really curious, I really care and want to know the answer." Because she seems so sincere, I will give her answers to difficult questions which, to be honest, sometimes surprise me. Like a good detective, there is nothing threatening in her questions, so my answers come easily and honestly.

If you can stop expecting to close the sale and practice active listening, you'll soon learn about the prospect's unmet needs. You'll discover which issues leave him frustrated and disappointed. You'll learn what things impress him, what makes his job easier, what makes him feel important. Chances are, he doesn't like to feel ignored or pushed. Not that you'd ever do that!

It's the Other 93 Percent That Can Kill Communication

Perceived threats aren't necessarily in the words, either. A recent study by Stanford University analyzed the way we communicate with each other. The study found that only 7 percent of our communication in a conversation comes from the words we speak. Thirty-eight percent came from the tone and inflection of our voices, and 55 percent came from our physiology or "body language."

When you're sitting in front of a prospect, it's not what you say but how you say it. When we agree with someone, we unconsciously "mirror" his posture. When we disagree, we assume an opposite stance. Closed physical gestures and expressions can convey a condescending, know-it-all, "I'm the sales king" attitude. Open postures and gestures can suggest the opposite — a very curious, "I really want to know" approach. If you can learn the latter, you will make it as easy as possible for the prospect to want to tell you the truth. And, as we all know, people do what they want, not what they should.

If you are truly interested in helping the prospect do what is best for him and his company, you will find it easy to help him in his process of self-discovery, to ask him questions that lead to self-surprising answers. If you are more interested in selling, pitching, and presenting, you won't. You will be pushing for an answer that you want to hear, one you already have in mind, and this pushing will keep the door closed on the very honesty and connections you need to succeed.

Find the Pain and Close More Deals

By establishing this dialogue, you will create a climate that promotes truth-telling and honesty. You will need that honesty to find the pain, hurts, wants, and needs that allow you to drive The Wedge.

We will talk more about the tactics used to set up The Wedge in the next section of this book. First, let me demonstrate why discovering the prospect's dissatisfaction (or "pain," as we call it) is absolutely vital to Driving The Wedge, busting up incumbent relationships, and closing more deals.

Fix It Or Forget It

In his outstanding book *Solution Selling*, Michael Bosworth points out that when people have a problem, they either fix it or forget it. For example, what would your company do if your accountant kept getting the math wrong and wasting company money? Why, they would fire her, of course! That's a direct "fix the pain" model.

> **Problem**....*Incompetent accountant.*
> **Result**.....*Pain in my pocketbook.*
> **Solution**...*Fire her and get someone competent.*

However, not all of life's problems are that easy to fix. Your agency, for example, may want an accountant who not only gets the numbers right, but also supplies weekly reports that are comprehensive, easy-to-read, and make economic forecasts about your company's revenues.

Not surprisingly, you may try several accountants and never find one whose work is completely satisfactory, or one who can help your company achieve its goals. Your firm may conclude that the level of service you want simply is not available and eventually settle on one accountant whose work is not completely satisfactory. The conclusion may be that this is just one of the insoluble problems of business and not worth wasting any more time worrying about.

Latent Memory Stores Forgotten Problems

In these cases, the dissatisfaction or pain as we will call it, is latent. Prospects don't wake up every morning and say, "Why can't I get my reports on time?" They just accept that timely reports are not available and carry on. The human mind does not like insoluble problems. It either finds an answer or forgets the problem, which is then stored in latent memory.

In an ideal world, every prospect will be sitting in his office when you arrive sighing "Thank God you're here! I've been looking for someone who can finally do these reports like I want them!" But that rarely happens. Instead, you must help your prospects along the path of self-discovery to uncover the latent pain they have forgotten.

If you can get your prospect to connect with you in an open and honest way, you can ask questions that can spur his latent memory and bring the pain to the forefront. To do so, your prospect has to believe that you might be able to do something about it. He must be convinced that you can be told this information without fear that you will use it against him.

Prospects Raise Walls

The prospect's fear — that the salesman will "use my pain against me to try and force me into a decision I don't want to make" — is the primary reason why prospects raise walls of dishonesty and insincerity with salespeople. This is one reason why the sales shark approach used by aggressive salespeople often fails. The prospect is the one with the problem and he wants to be in charge of implementing the solution. He certainly doesn't want to be pressured and berated by salespeople — even when they're right.

However, when you can overcome this fear and create an open, honest dialogue, you have the opportunity to jog the prospect's latent memory and bring up some of that unresolved pain. If the prospect is comfortable with you and believes you can be useful, he will share this pain with you, giving you the opportunity to drive The Wedge.

The Wedge at Work

Here is a sample conversation between a prospect and a salesperson representing a computer networking company. In it, you will see how pain is discovered, and then how it is used to drive The Wedge. (The comments in parentheses are the individual elements of The Wedge for reference later in the book.)

> **Salesperson:** *"About a year ago, I was working with the president of a company much like yours. One of his greatest concerns was the hassle and cost of borrowing money while waiting to collect his receivables. What he said he wanted was to reduce the time between shipping the product and getting paid. We were able to help him with that and as a result, he's reduced his lag time by eleven days and his costs of borrowing money are down 67 percent. . .Tell me about your situation."*

> **Prospect:** *"We've tried to accomplish the same thing. Our biggest challenge has been to get the information from our system to produce the invoices quickly."* (**Note:** *Anytime the prospect throws us a concern, we think of it as a softball and want to play catch. So we throw it back. Anytime a prospect throws you a "softball," it is the basis of a* **Reactive Wedge.***)*

> **Salesperson:** *"When you told the people you're dealing with that you weren't happy with the information from your system and that you wanted them to speed it up, I'm curious: What did they say?"*

Prospect: *"They said they would try to get us better and faster information."*

Salesperson: *"How's that going so far?"* (This is **Check Pulse.**)

Prospect: *"Nothing has really changed, I'm afraid."*

Salesperson: *"Well, maybe it's not that big a deal. After all, the cost of borrowing money is only a small fraction of your overhead."* (This is the **Take Away.**)

Prospect: *"Not exactly. We have some significant dollars tied up in there."*

Salesperson: *"Let me ask you this: When your current service provider came out and conducted a time-line analysis, and they looked at billing sources, how the information flows to your billing department, the speed with which invoices go out and the time it takes for those bills to be paid by your customers and to get that revenue into your system so that you could find the quickest path to get your cash back in and reduce your out-of-pocket expenses, were you comfortable with how they went through that analysis?"* (This is **Picture Perfect,** part of a **Proactive Wedge.**)

Prospect: *"Actually, uh, they didn't do that. To my knowledge, they don't even know how long it takes right now, or the impact of turning that information around more quickly."*

Salesperson: *"Well, maybe they have a long-term contract. They'll probably rise to the occasion when it's time to renew."* (**The Take Away**)

Prospect: *"That's crazy! We pay them a lot of money to do the best work possible. They should've handled this already."*

Salesperson: *"Do you want to talk about that?"*

Prospect: *"Sure."*

Salesperson: *"With regard to your billing and cash flow, what would you like to have happen?"* (This is the **Vision Box.**)

Prospect: *"Much like what you were talking about, I would like to cut our borrowing costs and the key to that is getting our billing out faster and reducing our collection time."*

Salesperson: *"Tell me, how much faster do you see as reasonable, and what effect do you believe that would have on your borrowing costs?"*

Prospect: *"I'm not really sure. I think it would be significant."*

Salesperson: *"OK, let's talk about how you see that happening. Would you want someone to do an analysis, a time-line of what is happening now?"*

Prospect: *"Yes, that makes sense to me."*

Salesperson: *"OK, who do you see involved in a project like this?"*

Prospect: *"I'd want Joe, he's our Finance Manager, and Sally, our I.S. Manager, and Jane in Operations."*

Salesperson: *"So, what I hear you saying is that what you need to get your revenue up is a computer system and strategy that will get reports out as soon as invoices come in, and that will also track those reports along with their status until the money comes in. Am I on the right track?"* (*This is the* **Replay.***)*

Prospect: *"Absolutely! Can you do it?"*

Salesperson: *"Sure. My company and I can do all of that for you. The technology exists, and we've done it for many companies like yours. That part is easy. I was wondering if we could deal with the hard part?"*

Prospect: *"What's that?"*

Salesperson: *"In a couple of days, I'll be back with a proposal that outlines how we can get this done. More than likely, you're going to look at it and say 'Yes, this is exactly what I want and these are the people I need to be dealing with.' The question is, when you decide that we are your new guys, how are you going to tell you current service providers that it's over? Because when you do, they're going to cry."* (*This is the* **Rehearsal.***)*

Prospect: *"Well, this is business. We'll just have to do what is best for us."*

Salesperson: *"Can you do that?"*

Prospect: *"I'm sure we can."*

Salesperson: *"Can I tell you what is going to happen?"*

Prospect: *"What's that?"*

Salesperson: *"When they hear that you really want this problem solved and that you are ready to make a change, your current rep is going to come over here. He'll tell you that if you'll give them another chance, they'll get it solved. He will ask to see my proposal and then do his best to convince you that they can do it. When he does that, how are you going to handle it?"*

Prospect: *"Hmmm...I see what you mean. I'll just have to tell him that....."*

Conclusion

As you can see, The Wedge deals directly with the problem of the incumbent, but it depends a great deal on the establishment of an honest rapport between you and your prospect. This honesty is essential if you are going to get the prospect to acknowledge her pain, and it also allows you to offer specific solutions to specific problems the prospect must solve to achieve her goals.

Focusing on the prospect's goals is an important part of moving away from "selling" and into winning. Focusing on the incumbent is also an important element because until the incumbent is dealt with, you cannot achieve your own goal of closing the deal. In fact, one could argue that the entire difference between "selling" and winning is in *your* focus.

When you focus on yourself and your company and you go into a sales call just slinging your best pitch, you are selling.

When you focus on your prospect and how you can help him achieve his goals by solving a specific problem, when you walk into the sales call prepared to anticipate those problems and offer specific solutions, then you start winning.

So, What Do I Do Now?

A quick recap:

- There are two problems that selling cannot solve:

    - The presence of the incumbent

    - The unwillingness of the prospect to talk to you honestly about his business.

- When it comes to dealing with the incumbent, The Laws of Physics are working against you:

    - No two objects can occupy the same space at the same time.

    - An object at rest tends to stay at rest.

    - For every action, there is likely to be an equal and opposite reaction.

- To overcome these conditions, you must bring an outside force to bear on the prospect/incumbent relationship. That force is the prospect's pain.

- "Pain" is short-hand for the dissatisfaction the prospect has with the service he is currently receiving from the incumbent rep, or for the desire the prospect has for a higher level of performance that has not yet been offered.

- The Wedge works by helping prospects discover for themselves their dissatisfaction, and then determining for themselves that you have the ability to resolve this pain and help them achieve more success for themselves and their companies.

Now that you understand the general concepts of The Wedge and what makes it work, the next three chapters will show you the techniques to use to create the right climate for using The Wedge in real life. If you learn these specific techniques, you will have more opportunities to drive The Wedge, break incumbent relationships, and give yourself the opportunity to close more deals.

Chapter Three

Knowing What You Don't Know:
How to Find, Analyze, and
Use Research to Turn Even
the Toughest Prospect
into a Winnable Deal

"It's not what you know, and it's not who you know, either. It's what you know about who you know that counts."

— Anonymous.

If you are like a lot of salespeople, you spend most of your time on the go. You're on the street, generating leads, making calls, dropping in on potential clients and servicing your existing accounts. You leave home early and come in late. You spend more time talking to your cell phone then you do your family. You make as many calls as you can because you have to. It's a numbers game, and your motto is "volume, volume, volume."

This approach allows very little time to find out much about your prospects. And it doesn't even acknowledge the existence of the number one deal-breaker, the incumbent. There is no strategy to put you, the producer, into an advantageous position against the incumbent, thereby increasing your odds of collecting a check.

For people who are selling, The Wedge is problematic because it forces you to slow down. It requires that you find out about both the prospect *and* the incumbent. It also requires that you do the research so you can walk into that sales call with a game plan that will let you close the deal.

In every sales game there are three primary players that need to be researched thoroughly:

- the prospective company and its internal players.
- the competition, particularly the incumbent agent you are competing against.
- the producer (you) and your company.

Easier said than done, yes? Research isn't easy, and it can be time-consuming. However, before you become discouraged, consider the many sources of quality information now available to you:

- your company and co-workers
- your prospective company and its employees
- vendors who serve the prospective company
- your other clients
- media, i.e., the Internet, news clippings, the library, etc.

Research Begins at Home

From the CEO's office to the mailroom, there are numerous places to research your prospects and competitors from right inside your own company.

Over the years, as I've coached producers in sales strategy meetings, there have been hundreds of occasions in which, as we detailed the prospect and her company, someone in the producer's own company knew something (or someone) that helped us advance our strategy. It's not uncommon, for example, for a fellow member of your sales team to have called on that prospect before and to have valuable information about the company's history or the prospect's personality and attitude.

Even if they're no longer employed, former producers from your firm can help. Sometimes former members of the sales staff will have left behind files or notes from their past pursuits of the prospect. I've even encountered situations where a new producer at my client's firm had worked at a competitive agency that wrote the business for a targeted prospect.

But nobody knew it, because nobody asked.

It is not uncommon for someone in your firm to attend the same church or be a member of the same club as a person that works at the prospective company. These personal contacts are excellent sources of information that can help you walk into your first meeting with a strategy to close.

Recently, I was working with a producer, strategizing on an account. The producer was in the employee benefits business, selling health insurance. I was surprised when in our discussion he told me that his brother-in-law was the vice president of sales in his prospective company. The producer had already met with the HR person that was responsible for buying health insurance for his company and had another meeting planned in a week.

This producer was relatively new in the employee benefits business but was a veteran of sales, having worked for another company for over ten years. His goal was to find out from the HR person what his needs and wants were and to learn about the company's decision-making process. From the outside looking in, you would have to wonder why this producer had not taken his brother-in-law out for dinner somewhere and obtained all of the inside scoop. His brother-in-law was more than willing to help in any way he could.

The first step to effective research in your sales office is communication within the agency. Be aggressive in asking for help, let your coworkers know what you're working on. Most of all, don't be a hero.

I've coached producers who literally refuse to ask members of their sales team for help. For whatever reason, they wanted their teammates to know as little as possible about their deals. Either they were afraid someone would steal their prospect, or they perceived it as a sign of weakness to ask for help. "That's for the new people," is the attitude I encountered, "not for experienced producers."

The sales game is not about being a hero, it's about winning. In the NBA, guys that want to be heroes and top scorers occasionally obtain those honors, but seldom do they win championships. Championships are won with *team* effort, obtaining and utilizing all the skills and information possible to win. There is a wealth of useful information inside your own company that can help you win more often. Learn how to use it.

Researching Inside
the Prospect's Company

When you research a prospect, your goal is to find information that will enable you to anticipate their problems and their needs, learn about their decision making process, and find out who the real players are and their relationship to any outside vendor incumbents. In doing this, you'll want to know what these people are trying to accomplish and what their corporate or business goals are so that you can bring the appropriate value from your company to help them achieve their goals.

In researching your prospect, you can often call other departments within the corporation to get information that will help your case. For example, you can call the marketing department and ask for a list of their top clients. In doing so, you can check to see if you share any clients. If so, you've discovered an excellent source of information.

And don't be shy about contacting the prospect company. Look for a reason for one of their salespeople to call on *you*, then use them to obtain inside information. The prospect's company probably has a public relations person whose job is to disseminate information. By all means, help them do their job!

I also recommend you try to find out who your prospect's boss is, as well as the names of any people who work for the prospect. In doing so, you've uncovered more people that someone you know, might know, too.

Check with Vendors, Clients, and Other Professionals

Depending on your business, your vendors might know a lot about your competition and, occasionally, about your prospects. These vendors derive revenue from you and your firm, so they are highly motivated to help you in any way they can. Get in the habit of finding out what other firms they work with.

Check with your clients as well. Any client in the same industry as your new prospect has probably at some time either competed against your prospect or worked with them. They might even be members of the same trade or professional association.

Think about the kinds of vendors all the people in your prospect's business are likely to share. It's not unusual, if you sell to niche markets, that an accounting firm will have made a decision to niche market as well. In a recent strategy session with a producer, he called one of his clients to find out who their CPA was. He found out that this CPA, being niche oriented, was the CPA for his prospect, too. Now, he has that internal connection with a knowledgeable vendor who wants to help. After all, CPAs need new business too.

On the Internet

Everyone can and should research prospects on the Internet. Your first stop is the company's official Web site, but it shouldn't be your last. If it's a publicly-traded company, you can find a good deal of financial information on sites designed for investors. In addition to basic facts, you'll find news releases that can tip you off to planned relocations, downsizing programs, new product launches, and potential take overs. All of these can tell you something about the firm's financial health and the sort of internal struggles that might impact the decision-maker with whom you plan to meet.

You can simply run a search and see what comes up. Just look at blog postings and message boards with a bit of healthy skepticism.

Then too, you can get personal. Check out the prospect in the local newspaper archives or business journal. Think of the impact you can make on a new prospect by quoting a comment he made in a recent interview in the business section. Not all of the half a billion Facebook users are teenagers. A lot of them are staid, solid professional companies and corporations. Check them out.

It's both exciting and frightening how much information is available from the public domain with just the click of a mouse. Internet research absolutely must be part of your preparation for meeting with prospects.

The Most Important Research Tool

The most important research tool is not a computer, a library or a friend who will dig through the prospect's trash can. *The most valuable tool is your willingness to ask for help.* Information is everywhere if you look. The more quality information you have the easier it is to drive The Wedge between your prospect and their incumbent agent.

Researching the Incumbent

When researching a prospect's business, one of the most important questions you want to answer is "Who is sitting in my chair." With a product such as insurance it's almost a certainty that there is an incumbent agent in place. Knowing who that is seems like common sense.

But it isn't. I'm astonished at the number of producers who call on prospects and have no idea who is already sitting in *their* chair. To me, it would be like dating a girl who has a boyfriend and not knowing who he is. If it's Hulk Hogan or The Rock, you don't want to find out that fact when you bump into him on your first date.

Finding out who the incumbent is should not be a problem. In insurance, as in most industries, there are a relative handful of top competitors and you can probably guess who's blocking you out at a particular company without even asking. It's like the NBA: There are only so many teams, and you're going to play the same ones several times a year. Learning who the superstars are isn't that difficult.

Amazingly, however, very few sales organizations keep up-to-date information on their competitors. It is very rare for me to go into a coaching session where the producers keep an active file on the people who are literally trying to kill their business and take bread off their table.

At the risk of being repetitive, let me remind you again: The Number One deal-breaker in every deal is the incumbent. As long as there is an incumbent, there is no prospect. You cannot close a deal until you break up the incumbent relationship, and the competing agent is going to do everything possible to prevent that.

Sales is a contact sport. Sales is not figure skating where you win or lose based on your performance. Sales is a game of ice hockey where you have to beat your opponent and drive him out of the box before you can score.

If you don't know anything about the agencies you're competing against, if you don't know what they offer or anything about their pricing structure, if you don't even know where they're located, you're not in a position to beat them.

How can you research your competitors? Once again, start with your sales team. They are competing against them every day. Ask your fellow producers about previous experiences they've had competing against the incumbent in question, successful and otherwise.

You may even want to create a common file for clippings, brochures, previous quotes and other information about competitors that you and your team come across. The process of gathering this information is valuable in and of itself because it focuses you on the third party in every deal — the incumbent.

When researching an incumbent, you want to know who they are, what they do, how long they have been the incumbent, and how they were able to get in. What is the nature of their relationship with the prospect? Is the prospect just a customer, buying from the incumbent the same way they buy bread at the store? Or is the prospect one of the incumbent's clients, someone they have a close, partner-like relationship with?

Researching Yourself to Find Your Advantage

My company, The Wedge Group, recently conducted a marketing research project on insurance agencies and made an interesting discovery. With almost no exception, all those we contacted marketed their agency in an identical manner emphasizing the following features: competitive pricing, commitment to quality, outstanding service, highly-trained staff, and a solid reputation. Every agency claimed that these features made them different from their competitors.

At the conclusion of our research, I made the determination that the so-called "marketing efforts" used by most of these agencies were failing because what they thought were their strengths were really the minimum acceptable standards for being in business. In other words, what these agencies thought made them "better" really made them the same as everybody else.

When we looked at the major insurance companies, we found that they were to a great degree offering the same services and products at competitive prices. The insurance agencies representing these major insurance companies were in fact representing even more sameness.

Excellence has become the minimum standard for business in America's competitive workplace. Meeting these high standards has turned every producer into a cheerleader for the same quality level of products and services.

What does this mean to you? It means that if you're selling features and benefits, you're losing, because dozens of your competitors are working the same prospects and selling the same things in the same way. And if you and the incumbent are essentially the same, why should the prospect go through the pain of making a change?

This is where researching your own agency becomes vitally important. Whether you sell property and casualty or life and health, chances are you and your competitors are offering very similar products and services. The difference isn't in what you do, but how you do it. *It isn't your products' features or benefits you need to sell, but how you deliver those products and services in a way that makes a difference for the prospect.*

Your challenge is to research what you do and how you do it in order to find your strengths. Once you do that you'll be prepared when you meet with a prospect to compare your strengths to your competition's weaknesses.

Strength vs. Weakness

You are in a game against your competitor, the incumbent, a game that you want to win. The incumbent agent only has to tie, or may even be able to score a little less, because he has a relationship with the prospect that you don't have.

If you haven't compared your strengths against the incumbent's weaknesses in advance, what's going to happen? You may mention the area of well-trained staff, for example, only to find out that the incumbent's staff is equally well trained. Your strength vs. his strength: It's a wash. And since, as they say in baseball, "a tie goes to the runner," you lose.

You may demonstrate clearly that you have a fast turn-around time, only to find out that the incumbent is faster. Your weakness vs. his strength: You lose again.

43

What you need, as the new producer competing against the incumbent, is to match your strengths versus her weaknesses. That is the only winning match-up where you have the advantage.

You		Incumbent	Result
Strength	vs.	Strength	Wash (You lose)
Weakness	vs.	Strength	You Lose
Strength	vs.	Weakness	Your Advantage

No matter what sport you follow or how big a fan you are, when two teams which are evenly matched meet, a good game is almost certain. But not guaranteed. Sometimes injuries tip the scale; sometimes it all comes down to who wants it more. Sometimes, however, a star wide receiver lines up opposite a Pro Bowl strong safety and nothing happens. No completions. No yardage. No scores. Unless the offensive coordinator switches to his running game, you've got a snoozer on your hands. Send an ace pitcher against a strong hitter and it's a walk instead of a home run. And a great point guard can neutralize a power forward. In all of these cases, strength cancels out strength. The team that will win is the one that can play to the opponent's weakness.

The thing is, in sports and life, you can't be good at everything. Your agency is great at some things, good at some things and average at others. The same is true for your competitor, the incumbent. Because most producers work for agencies that do essentially the same things, you must find *how* what you do is different and consequently better. This may seem like a strange concept, but before you meet with a prospect, it's vital that you know what you do well, how you do it, what kinds of problems you can solve, and how quickly. You need to be prepared to focus your conversation with the prospect on areas where you and your company are strong and the competition is weak.

Not every producer agrees with me, by the way. Many of them assume that, since they and the incumbent offer essentially the same thing, all they need to do is offer "the same service at a better price!" They are wrong, and they would realize how wrong if they started keeping track of how often they get "rolled" by the incumbent.

That's because you can never offer exactly the same product as the incumbent, ever. If you match your competitors feature for feature, service for service, you still lose because you can never offer the one exclusive product of the incumbent: an existing relationship with the prospect.

The incumbent has one. You don't.

To break apart that incumbent relationship, you must put your strength against the incumbent's weakness. This is why research is vitally important. Without it, how will you know which services and products to promote when you meet with the prospect? How else can you make strategic decisions before your sales call so you can drive The Wedge which will give you the winning advantage?

The Real Test of Your Research

Look in your appointment book for an upcoming prospect meeting on your schedule. Ask yourself these questions:

- Who in the company will make the final decision to hire me?
- Who do I know in the company that knows these people?
- Do my fellow producers know anyone who knows these people?
- What are the most common problems in this company's industry?
- What are the specific problems or issues inside this company that my prospect is trying to address?
- Who is the incumbent agent?
- What are the three things I do better than the incumbent?

- What questions can I ask the prospect that will help him clearly see that we are the better choice?
- What are the three things my agency and I do better than anyone else?

These are just a few of the questions you should have concrete, rehearsed answers to before you walk into a prospect meeting. There are many more, and I urge you to develop your own list of what's important. I also encourage you to retain this valuable information and update it from time to time. Every contract comes up for renewal eventually, and key contacts and decision-makers leave or are promoted to new responsibilities. Things change. That's why your research file also must be dynamic.

The key question on research is this: Do you have a strategy to win the research game? Until you do, you are fighting a losing battle. Your time, effort and research can guarantee you an opportunity to close every deal, if you have the winning Wedge.

Chapter Four

Rapport: Creating an Environment for Truth-Telling

One of the two great challenges facing every producer is the prospect's unwillingness to tell the truth. There are several reasons why, not the least of which is the fact that by suggesting he make a change, you are challenging a previous decision. The quickest way to get people to be defensive is to tell them that the decisions they've made were wrong.

Therefore, before you make your sales call, you need a strategy that you can use to create a climate of truthfulness in your face-to-face meeting. You want to make it easy for the prospect to be honest about his or her company, goals, even his or her mistakes. It won't be easy.

Before a prospect will be honest with you, she must be comfortable with you and believe that you are able to help. *These are the two tests: credibility and comfort.* Until you pass these two tests, it is unlikely that you will have an open, honest dialogue with the people you call on.

When I am training people to use The Wedge, I refer often to Michael Brooks' book, *Instant Rap-*

---

6 *Reasons Why Prospects Don't Tell the Truth*

1. *They don't like you.*
2. *They don't trust you.*
3. *They don't want to look stupid by admitting their mistake.*
4. *They have another relationship to protect.*
5. *They are on a "power trip" to compensate for low self esteem.*
6. *You are showing your sales technique.*

---

port, for strategies that will create an environment in which the prospect is *willing* to tell you the truth. Rapport helps you quickly create a relationship based on comfort and credibility. You want your prospect to be comfortable speaking with you honestly, and you want him to believe that if he tells you his problem, you can do something about it.

Taking this approach, you can see that the entire burden for creating effective communication is on you. It's your job to find out what you need to know. You can't count on the prospect to tell you. In a new business sales interview, you're the one who wants something, therefore, you are the one responsible for establishing rapport. You must be flexible and willing to make shifts in body posture and the speed and tone of your voice, as well as to adjust your emotional state to match that of your prospect.

How to Establish Rapport

There is an old cliché that states, "When in Rome, do as the Romans do." What does that mean? Does it mean you need to dress like they dress, talk like they talk, sit like they sit, like what they like? Yes, to a great degree. What you will find to be true is that people like people who are most like themselves. The more two people share in common, the greater the degree of rapport.

Do different situations, people, or places make you feel at least a little uncomfortable? Of course they do. On the other hand, do you generally feel comfortable with that which you consider normal, or just like you? Most people do. So the question is, how do you consistently create an environment where people feel comfortable? One way is for you to mimic what is normal for them.

I was working with a young woman who had been in sales for about one year. She had been taught to always sit up straight as an arrow with both feet planted firmly on the floor. Her posture was so erect that she looked almost uncomfortable. In her new job, she was calling on small business owners of manufacturing facilities. She would go into a call all prim, proper, and professional to meet with a guy that didn't wear a tie, sat back in his chair a little slumped with one leg crossed over the other.

She already had a couple of strikes against her for being young and not having much in common with her prospects, but she accentuated those differences by the way she sat and talked. If her goal was to create an environment where her prospect felt comfortable and talked openly, she probably wasn't going to achieve that goal. So what could she have done differently?

Match and Mirror

There are many areas in which you can create rapport. One area is simply by talking about things that you share with the prospect. We call this *conscious* rapport, because you consciously make a decision to pick out something as a point of conversation such as a photo or picture hanging on the wall or an object on the prospect's desk. Even though the effort is obvious (conscious), it's a nice way to break the ice and form an area of commonality.

But what kind of effect is there on your prospect when you adjust the speed of your voice to match his? What about when you adjust the way you sit to provide a mirror image of your prospect? The answer is *subconscious rapport*. By matching their voice, the speed and tone, as well as mirroring their body posture, your prospects will feel much more comfortable with you and not really know why. If asked, they would just say, I like her and felt comfortable with her. But, more than likely wouldn't know why.

These rapport strategies are powerful tools. They will enable your prospect to get comfortable with you more quickly, which will lead to a willingness to be more vulnerable and to talk about what is really important — his goals, dreams and desires for his company and for himself.

I once had a meeting with a gentleman almost twenty-five years my senior. He was a typical Texan in that he talked with a drawl — kind of slow and easy going. We were having breakfast one morning at a hotel in Dallas and I began the conversation with a very active "Match and Mirror" strategy: slowing the speed of my voice down to match his, sitting back in my chair very relaxed, just like him. The comfort level was high and the level of truth-telling was significant.

However, as the conversation progressed, I could see the opportunity for us to get a $700,000 contract that would generate a $70,000 fee for us. The more that fee became a reality, the more excited I began to get. This excitement (not to mention the effect of three cups of coffee) began to work against me.

I went from mirroring his posture and matching the speed and tone of his voice, to sitting up, leaning forward, and talking faster. That response is normal for me, particularly when I am closing in on a $700,000 deal, but it wasn't normal for him. In fact, it nearly cost me the deal.

Why? The reason I had a great chance of getting that deal in the first place was because our intimate level of rapport had allowed him to talk openly about his current dissatisfaction, his *pain*. He had problems that needed solutions. That was his emotional state.

Meanwhile, my emotional state had shifted to one of excitement. To him, it appears that the longer he talks about his unhappiness, the happier I become. It took me a few minutes to notice, but as I was becoming excited, he was becoming turned off. I had mismatched his emotional state as well as mismatching his posture and voice. Where before there was harmony, there was now disharmony.

I finally noticed how his body posture had shifted away from me when I was sitting up. He seemed to cower a bit, as if to say: "Back off, buddy." When I recognized what was going on, I slowly, but deliberately, made a shift back to matching him. I sat back and slowed my voice from excited to matching his "concerned" state of mind, and then he made his shift. We were back in harmony and rapport was reestablished.

Here is an example of how match and mirror works in your own life. Have you ever had "one of those days?" You know, the days when, from the time you get up and stub your toe on the closet door until you come rushing into the office late after sitting in traffic all morning, nothing goes right? Maybe you're just in a foul mood, or you've forgotten your wife's birthday. Well, the only thing worse than "one of those days" is having it interrupted by "Happy Bob."

Happy Bob (or "Babs") is the person at your office whose core philosophy of life is that everybody should be happy. When Happy Bob encounters an unhappy coworker, he feels like it's his job in life to cheer her up. He's always got a cartoon clipped out of some "Perky People" monthly magazine, or he's downloaded Letterman's Top Ten list from the night before. Whatever it takes, he wants you to be happy.

When you're in a good mood, Happy Bob is a pleasant enough person to be around. But on "one of those days," you want to grab his "Don't Worry, Be Happy!" paperweight and shove it down his throat. The mismatch of your emotional states leads you to the brink of violence.

To a lesser degree, the same is true during a sales call. People like people who are like themselves. If the person you are calling on is in a high spirited, cheerful mood, raise your level to match it. However, if your prospect is much more reserved and quiet, don't try to make a party out of it. Match them and you will have much greater rapport.

Increasing your ability to establish a greater level of rapport by matching and mirroring is very important to getting out of the selling cycle and into the winning cycle. One of the primary keys to winning is quality information, the kind that can and will make the difference in the deal.

Creating Credibility

Matching and mirroring helps create rapport by creating comfort, by actively seeking paths of connection at the conscious and subconscious level. It is a pragmatic, easy-to-use technique that you can immediately put to work in your sales calls.

However, there is another essential element of truth-telling: credibility. Once again, the prospect must be comfortable enough to tell you the truth and believe you can do something about it once he tells you. Modeling will make him comfortable. How can you make yourself credible in his eyes? You can create credibility with a story.

If you've done even a minimal amount of research before your sales call, you should have a fairly accurate picture as to where the prospect's company is when you walk into the office: what they are trying to achieve, and what problems they need to solve. If you're lucky, you may also enter the meeting with some research about the individual prospect: Is she a sales shark who was brought in to double the company's volume, or is she a newly-promoted executive whose highest priority is demonstrating competence in her new position?

Regardless of the situation, you should be prepared with a powerful, well-rehearsed story regarding a third party who was in a situation similar to that of the prospect. This referral story should demonstrate that you have a clear understanding of the prospect's business, have worked with a similar business to solve an important problem — one the prospect is likely to face, and that you are capable of doing the same today.

Stories work because they allow you to communicate without selling. When you're selling, you are either talking about yourself ("Our company has been a leader in the industry for..."), or you are cross-examining the prospect ("Have you or your company ever had a problem with..."). Neither of these create rapport or a climate for truth-telling. In fact, you are either boring the prospect by making the same pitch all of your competitors make, or you are making him defensive about decisions made in the past.

Telling a story lets you share information about your competence and your company's features without slinging sales talk at your prospect. It gives you a chance to demonstrate in very specific language how the products or services you offer have benefited people like the prospect, to let him see you in action, if you will.

If you've done your research, you will be prepared with a story about a similar third party. An outline of such a story might look like this:

1. *"It's been my experience working with other companies in this industry..."* A broad outline of the current situation in the prospect's industry allows you to demonstrate your general familiarity with the marketplace.

2. *"The (owner/manager) of one of the companies I have worked with was concerned about..."* A specific problem that you have helped solve for others and based on your research is likely to be a significant issue with this prospect.

3. *"When I spoke to the [owner/manager/etc.], what he wanted was..."* A solution to the problem listed previously.

4. *"We were able to ..."* A simple statement that says "we gave him the solution."

5. *"As a result..."* List the concrete rewards in terms of time or money saved.

6. *"Now, tell me about your situation."* Find out about the prospect's situation.

You have now given the prospect a clear and specific scenario in which you helped a company in her situation solve a specific problem, and you did it in language that demonstrated your familiarity with her industry. You have immediately started establishing credibility. Your prospect now knows that you understand her industry, business, and potential problems or concerns.

Moreover, when you started talking about the solutions your previous client wanted, you raised the question in your prospect's mind: "Are these solutions affordable or even doable?" By going next to "We gave them those solutions and as a result, reduced their cost of ____ and saved time on ____.", you answered that question and raised another in the prospect's mind: "Can you do this for me?"

So, when you close with "Tell me about your situation," your prospect wants to talk about his current circumstances to get the answer to his question. You have accomplished your goal: the prospect wants to communicate and to do so honestly.

The goal of your story is clear: create comfort and establish credibility. The tactic is simple. Tell a story that will resonate with the prospect, highlighting your proven ability to help other people like him solve their problems.

To recap let's go over the credibility and triggering technique:

- Stated Concerns
- Solutions Wanted
- Solutions Given
- Positive Past Results Presented
- Credibility created by showing that you understand your prospect's business and potential concerns
- Concerns transformed into the specific outcomes and solutions wanted
- Hope created in the prospect's mind — "If they solved it, maybe we can too"
- Results quantified in concrete and specific time and money saved

Do you have a list of your best business stories? I do. And most of the highly successful producers I've worked with do too. Some of them write down every word (with stage directions.) But most of them just keep an informal list with a key word or two to trigger the example that best illustrates the point they are trying to make. Finding and refining these real-life examples will help you to relate to your prospects because your relaxed familiarity with the story will make it feel more natural rolling off your tongue. It therefore will be more convincing to the listener.

Chapter Five

Discovery: No Pain, No Change

So, you've done your research and are more confident with your ability to fight the battles in areas where you have strengths and your competition has weaknesses. You now know more about your prospect's business and have a definitive path to make a real difference. You've sharpened your rapport building skills and have a strategy to encourage honest discussion with your prospect. Now you need to discover those issues that will motivate your prospect to make changes.

What is it you are looking for? In a word, pain.

Pain, loosely defined here as dissatisfaction, disappointment or unresolved tension, is an essential part of The Wedge. In fact, if you cannot find your prospect's pain, you will not be able to drive The Wedge, move the incumbent and close the deal. It truly is a case of "No pain, no change."

This is particularly true when selling commercial insurance. If you can't help your prospect identify and acknowledge dissatisfaction with his current agent, you have virtually no chance of getting a shot at winning.

Even if you are offering a better price, there is an 80 percent likelihood that your prospect will somehow give his current (the incumbent) agent a chance to stay in the game by matching the deal. And in most cases, because it's cheaper to discount a little than it is to find a new customer, the incumbent agent will match your price (or come close) and keep the business.

Remember, change is painful. If there is no pain, no dissatisfaction, no unfulfilled expectation, then why would a prospect want to go to the trouble of establishing a new relationship, taking a chance that things might even get worse over time. This is particularly true when, with a phone call or a meeting, they could probably use the competing agent's quote as leverage to get their existing agent to lower their price.

So the million dollar question is, "How do you find pain? Where do you look?"

Finding the Pain

What makes an FBI investigator so good at finding the clues at the scene of the crime? He knows where to look. If they put you or me out there looking for clues we'd probably be going in circles in just moments. At the FBI Academy, they have a special course on how to find clues. In sales we should have a course on how to find pain, because that is the primary difference between *selling* and *winning*.

A seller will go into a new business sales appointment ready to tell the company story. The winner will go into a new business sales interview looking for the prospect's pain.

Where Does Pain Reside?

Think of your mind as a computer. The things you see on the monitor screen represent the things in "the front of your mind," the RAM or random access memory of the computer. Just as your computer's memory can only handle six or seven programs at a time, your active memory can only handle thinking about six or seven issues at once. Call it multi-tasking. No matter how good you are at it, even you have limitations.

In addition to its RAM, your computer also has a hard drive that can store vast amounts of information that it can recall on demand. Millions of bytes of information sit dormant at all times, waiting for the right keystrokes to call them onto your screen into the computer's active memory.

This is a good analogy for what goes on inside our minds. Think for a moment about what is happening when you walk into a prospect's office for a sales call. The prospect is usually up to his ears in activity: an employee quit that morning, the P&L just came out and needs to be reviewed, one of the kids has a soccer game at 5:30, and the printer just ate the report that is due tomorrow morning. His active memory is full of all these current events that are taking up space.

Now, if you happen to be in the business of solving one of these specific, immediate problems, you're in luck! You are likely to hear: "I'm glad you're here. I have this problem, can you help me?"

However, if your prospect doesn't have an immediate problem related to insurance, then you're going to have a difficult time getting his attention. So what do you do? You can ask the basic questions such as "Got any problems?" and "How are things going?" but you're unlikely to get a useful response.

This doesn't mean that there aren't any problems. It just means that you haven't pulled them up from the prospect's latent memory (his "hard drive") and into his active memory (onto the "screen"). The information is there, but hidden. You need the right set of "key strokes" or questions to bring it up and into the prospect's consciousness.

Fix It or Forget It

There are two human reactions when confronted with a problem: either find a solution (which involves the active memory), or set the problem aside until a satisfactory solution can be found (which means storing the problem in your latent memory). If you are capable of solving the problem, the problem is gone and the experience is mentally filed away as complete. On the other hand, if the problem cannot be solved for whatever reason — too expensive, no immediately definable solution, too much trouble — then the problem is forgotten, filed away in your latent memory.

So all of life's unsolved problems are stored in the latent memory. As a salesperson, you have to know what those problems are likely to be and have a solution if you expect to reach your prospects at this level.

How Do You Know What Someone's Problem Is until You Ask?

Problems are like center stripes in the highway — they repeat themselves. If you have found a common problem among clients, it is reasonable to expect that most of your prospects will share the same problem. Although you won't know for sure until you ask, you can make that assumption and, if it calls up a reaction from the prospect's latent memory, confirm your assumption.

Some examples of the kinds of problems that people tend to store in their latent memory might include baldness, fear of public speaking, being overweight, or having poor eyesight. On a day-to-day basis, if you asked these people how they are doing, they would respond "Fine, just fine!" If you asked if they had any personal problems they needed help with, they would likely say no.

But imagine if you mentioned to your friend with male pattern baldness that you had just found a product that grew hair instantly, what would be the response? "Really? You found a cure for baldness?"

Five minutes ago, he had no problems. Everything was fine. Now you are about to become a hero. Why? The problem was always there, but you presented the possibility of a solution.

Creating Pain (The Proactive Wedge)

When you meet with a prospect who, even after rapport is established, does not share any pain with you, don't be fooled into thinking all of his problems have been solved. There are often times

58

when it will seem the prospect isn't looking for solutions because he does not perceive that he has a problem. This doesn't mean things are perfect, far from it. It is just as likely that the prospect believes that things are as good as they're going to get, that the problems he faces are like the weather conditions that must be dealt with but cannot be changed.

This prospect is in the forget it stage. Ongoing problems that could not be solved have been relegated to his latent memory. Since a person's active memory can only remember approximately seven items at the same time, it stores intractable or seemingly unsolvable problems in latent memory.

Thus the strategy you develop before you meet with the prospect isn't to *create* pain, but to uncover unresolved problems from the prospect's latent memory. This is the purpose of the **Proactive Wedge**.

One important element for uncovering pain in the latent memory is using the "Picture Perfect" technique. We will cover **Picture Perfect** in more detail in Chapter 7, but from a preparation standpoint, your goal is to enter the meeting with a clear, well-conceived image of the ideal circumstances under which the prospect could be doing business, one that you can provide. You want to paint a word picture of perfection itself, of how things could be working for the prospect.

Here's an example. Let's say you have an assistant or customer service representative assigned to you. Your colleague shares the services of another CSR with two other sales reps. What kind of a response do you think you would get if you said: "You know, I couldn't close my next sale if I didn't have Emily behind me. When I come in on Monday morning, she brings my coffee and all the relevant files like in a doctor's office. Everything's at my fingertips. She knows all my key accounts by name and their assistants. She asks what I want for lunch on the days I'm here and where she should make reservations on the days I'm not. Sometimes she even drops off and picks up my dry cleaning when I need it. Last month, she helped me with a gift for my wife's birthday. I sure like this idea of having a dedicated CSR. How's it working out for you?"

The answer you're likely to get back is: "What planet do you live on? I'm lucky if my assistant returns phone calls. Are you serious? Does your assistant really do all that?"

You've just created space between the incumbent and the prospect by getting the prospect to see the difference between what he has and what he *could* have. You've sown the seeds of dissatisfaction: the beginning of a **Proactive Wedge**.

You should enter each sales call with several examples of **Picture Perfect** service that can be used to bring up unresolved or unrealized dissatisfaction. Obviously, you will be looking for spontaneous acknowledgments of pain, but you can't just hope to get lucky. You have to develop your own strategies to create pain, to give yourself opportunity after opportunity to **Drive the Wedge**.

You want to enter your meetings thoroughly prepared and researched, and you want to create a credible, comfortable climate for the prospect to share any of the problems she's got in the front of her mind with you. You always want to look for spontaneous pain and a **Reactive Wedge**.

However, it's possible that there may not be any. That's when Proactive Wedges become useful. Proactive Wedges are educated guesses about what the prospect's concerns and problems are likely to be. They raise issues that, from your research, you would reasonably expect to lead to dissatisfaction on the part of a prospect.

Here's an example: You are talking to a prospect about your previous work for a similar company, and you bring up the issue of claims.

> **Producer:** *"...and that's what he wanted done so that he could reduce his cost of claims. By the way, I'm curious, when your current agent came out at the end of the first quarter to go through your loss runs with you and he went through the open claims with you looking for the one's where the reserve was set too high, then developed a plan of action to get them reduced, so you wouldn't have to worry about paying for your insurance. Were you comfortable with how he went through that process?"*

> **Prospect:** *"Uh, actually I don't recall him having done that."*

Producer: *"Well, maybe it's not that important because you never have any medium or large size claims."*

Prospect: *"Well sure we do, it happens occasionally."*

Producer: *"OK. Can I put that one on the shelf for a moment? Let me ask you this; when your current agent came out after renewal to help you set up your safety meetings and he brought out a list of videos available, helped you set up a meeting schedule and a method to document your meetings so you wouldn't have to worry about OSHA fines or wasting money on preventable injuries, how did that go?"*

Prospect: *"Frankly, my agent doesn't do that either."*

Producer: *"Hmmm. Doesn't it make sense to talk about those things?"*

Prospect: *"Sure."*

Producer: *"OK, in regards, to managing your claims and having more effective safety meetings, what would you like to have happen?"*

Prospect: *"I'm not really sure. I do know that I'd like to get more proactive in trying to reduce the cost of our claims."*

Producer: *"OK, who all would be involved in that sort of an ongoing project?"*

Prospect: *"My shop foreman, HR manager, and the CFO. (**Vision Box***)"*

And **The Wedge** is driven.

Notice that this script assumes that the prospect never mentioned any problems, and that, if you had asked the question: "Are you satisfied with your agent's service," the answer would likely have been positive.

What the Proactive Wedge does is to assume that the prospect has had claims problems before (a fairly safe assumption) and then presents a scenario of **Picture Perfect** service that would solve the problem. If the prospect has had these problems, you will jog his latent memory. He should be very interested in what you present. If he doesn't, you can go onto another **Proactive Wedge** and get another opportunity to find pain and remove the incumbent.

Remember that analogy about you and the computer memory? We all know what happens to our work when the power unexpectedly goes out. Your computer remembers what is stored on the hard drive. What is new in its active memory is susceptible to loss unless or until it is saved. You may remember every Wedge you ever used... or you may not. I hope you're writing yours down somewhere for future reference. Because your ability to repeat your sales success is key to achieving your career success.

Chapter Six

Differentiation:
How You Do What You Do
Better Than Anyone Else

One of my clients, an enthusiastic young producer who had just gotten into the business of selling commercial insurance, made an astonishingly obvious, but important, observation in front of his training group. Speaking with the arrogance of youth, he announced: "I *know* I can do a better job for my clients. I've just got to get them to know it, too!"

If enthusiasm made successful producers, America would be awash in millionaires. But energy and desire, while important, won't accomplish your goal. Beating out the incumbent agent will. To achieve your goal, you must do four things (three of which we've already covered):

- Know What You Don't Know (**Research**)
- Create an Atmosphere for Truth-Telling (**Rapport**)
- Have a Strategy to Find Pain (**Discovery**)

And like the ambitious young producer described in the first paragraph,

- Get the Prospect to See How We Can Do a Better Job, Too. (**Differentiation**)

There is no step more vital in the sales game than developing a strategy to differentiate yourself from all the other companies and other producers who are offering nearly identical products and services at nearly identical prices. It is a prime reason why we do research on ourselves and our own companies, and it is the reason why we are focusing on it at length in this chapter.

Let's go back to the **Picture Perfect** customer service representative that I used in Chapter 5. It effectively illustrates several concepts, including the value of words that are specific and concrete.

For example, let's try the same conversation this way: "You know, I love having an assistant. My CSR is always doing things for me that make my workday easier. Don't you like having that kind of support?" Same story, but what sort of response will you get this time, strained credulity? No. Chances are the answer would be "Sure! She holds down the fort so I can be out making calls."

What happened? You just said the same thing, but in a different way. You took a very specific, concrete, image-filled description of an *ideal* assistant and reduced it to an abstract generalization. By doing so, you took all the power of differentiation out of your words. Your CSR sounds just like your friend's, so how could he perceive the difference?

Now, let's bring the principle of differentiation back to the real world of sales:

During a sales coaching seminar, one of my favorite exercises as a sales strategist and motivator is to get them talking about why their company or agency is better than the competition.

"Agencies are as different as night and day," I tell them. "The services, the people and the way they provide service are vastly different. Please take a moment to list at least four areas where your company is different or better than your competitors."

The people who attend my workshops are obviously motivated and intelligent, and in a few minutes we have a long list of outstanding features: the latest technology, well-trained employees, commitment to quality service, a solid reputation in the industry, strong relationships with our markets — the list goes on and on.

Then I present the list their competitors would write and, inevitably, they are identical. Why?

Because as we pointed out earlier, in almost every industry today, the features listed above aren't exceptional, they are the *minimum* standard for doing business. Every company, particularly the major players you're likely to be competing against, is working hard to keep up with new technologies and is using strategies like Team Building to increase productivity and improve customer satisfaction.

Therefore, being different from your competitors is not a function of the differences in the firms themselves but in the people representing them — the producers. Your sales style, your ability to cause clients to think critically and perceive a positive difference between your firm and any other, are qualities that are much more vital to success than proving that your company is "better," based on some arbitrary level of service or the perceived quality of your reputation.

> *Remember, among quality, competitive companies, there will be little difference in features or benefits. Listing your company's features merely meets the minimum requirements of doing business and makes you sound like everyone else. The key element is not your product or service: It's You!*

So, if you and your competitors are providing essentially the same services, how do you differentiate between yourself and your competitors?

It's not what you do, it's how you do it — the process by which you provide your service. This is where you can set your company apart from the competition and create the opportunity for differentiation.

Think of your favorite clothing store. Go to any mall in America, and there are probably dozens of stores that offer the same clothes for about the same price. So what sets your favorite store apart from the rest?

It's the process. It begins when you walk in the door. It's how you're greeted, it's the way the sales clerks size you up, the way they ask you what you are looking for and where you plan to wear it. When you leave the store, you leave with a suit or dress that you could have purchased anywhere. But because of the quality of the process, you chose to buy it from this store and, chances are, you'll be back again. The difference is not in the product, it's in how the product is delivered.

Now think about yourself and your agency. How do you deliver your product in a way that is different from your competition? We know that the products and services are about the same — so what's different?

Let's return to the example of the clothing store. Every store has clothes, they all have salespeople, they have sales, they take returns — these are the bare bones requirements of being in the clothing business. If this store ran an ad campaign saying "Come to our clothing store! We're different, we have clothes!" you would think that was strange.

But that's precisely how you sound when you sit down with a prospect and start listing the features of your company, features shared by every company in the business. Who doesn't claim to offer "quality service?" What company doesn't strive for "competitive prices?"

These features are the bare bones of your business. Your job is to put meat on those bones, to flesh out an image of your company that gives your prospect a detailed and attractive picture of what you can offer. And the bones you want to flesh out are the processes of providing the common services that set you apart.

The first step on your path from selling to winning is to take your focus off the features of your product or service and to zero-in on the way you and your company *provide* service, which is the one area where your differences are most likely to stand out.

Sounds simple, right? Unfortunately, simplicity is probably your biggest obstacle.

Climbing Down the Ladder of Abstraction

Think about the words we've been using to describe the characteristics of your company or agency: quality service, new technology, competitive pricing, customer orientation. All of these words share a characteristic among themselves. They are abstract.

Abstract concepts like love, hate, humanity, quality, competition, and technology are difficult to visualize. What does "love" look like? Can you draw a picture of "quality?" And if you can't do it, neither can your prospect. If your prospect can't picture what you are offering, she will never see the difference between you and the incumbent.

For your prospect to see the differentiation, you must project concrete, easy-to-see images of the service you provide. You do this by climbing down the *ladder of abstraction*.

The concept of the ladder of abstraction comes from linguist and former U.S. Senator S.I. Hiyakowa. In his famous book, *Language In Thought and Action*, he puts the language we use on a scale, from abstract to concrete, and uses the ladder as a metaphor to help us choose what level of language we should use.

For example: you are driving to a sales call and pass a cow standing in field. When you get to your appointment, you might say: "You know what I saw on the way here? A mammal." Or you could say "I saw Farmer Brown's black cow, Bessie." In both cases, you would be accurate. But the phrase that allows the listener to visualize most precisely what you are describing is "Farmer Brown's black cow, Bessie."

The phrase works because it is concrete, it is at the bottom of the ladder of abstraction. Moving up the ladder, you could say you saw "one of Farmer Brown's cows;" "a Hereford;" "a cow;" "a farm animal;" "a mammal;" "a quadruped;" "a life form;" "something."

Each rung of the ladder describes Bessie, just at a different level of abstraction. Your goal when describing how your company provides its services is to stay as low on the ladder as possible. Telling me you offer "time-sensitive service" does not help me visualize what you will do for me. But letting me know that you guarantee "twenty-four-hour turn-around" gives me a clear picture, one that I can compare with the incumbent.

Here's another example:

It's time for lunch, and you walk down to the corner where there are two restaurants: Abner's Abstract Grill and Cathy's Concrete Cafe. You stick your head in at Abner's and ask "What's good today?" Abner sticks his head out of the kitchen and says "The burgers are very good today. You'll like 'em!"

You walk across the street to Cathy's and ask her the same thing. Cathy says: "I just finished grinding the fresh sirloin for our burgers—it's 98 percent fat-free and ready to flame-broil on our mesquite grill, which is designed to sear in all the juices. We season it with a special blend of Worcestershire, black pepper, and garlic and serve it hot and fresh on a whole wheat sesame seed bun, along with a heaping order of gourmet onion rings."

I ask you: which restaurant makes a better burger? The fact is, Abner's Abstract Grill might prepare his burgers exactly the same way… even better! But because he doesn't relate it in a way that allows you to visualize the qualities of his product, it's just "good." But what does good taste like?

If you want your prospect to see the differences between you and your competitors, you must be prepared with well-rehearsed stories and images that avoid abstract phrases that merely meet the minimum standard of service. You want to focus on the way you deliver these services and use concrete images to help your prospect visualize the differences between you and your competitors.

If you will use concrete language to help your prospect visualize the way you provide services, you will increase your opportunity to create differentiation and to break apart the incumbent relationship.

Abstract vs. Concrete: The Wedge at Work

Suppose you are the CFO of a medium size manufacturing firm and you have plans to meet with two agents from different insurance agencies.

The agent from agency A sits down and does a few things to establish rapport. Then he starts telling you about his company—its reputation and commitment to quality service. Soon he goes into his presentation about their service standards, number of markets, and risk management philosophy and asks you for an opportunity to provide a competitive quote.

The agent from agency B comes in, and after doing a few things to establish rapport, she begins with a brief story to gain some credibility. She then asks a few questions:

Producer: *"During a meeting with the executives of a medium size manufacturing firm, the CFO told me his greatest concern was that all of the services available to him were poorly coordinated and because of that he didn't feel he was getting all that he was paying for. What he said he wanted was a more defined annual service plan that was proactive in nature and would help him exercise maximum control to prevent and manage losses. We gave him that and as a result his cost of losses has decreased by over 37 percent. Tell me about your situation."*

Prospect: *"That's been a significant challenge. I don't have the time to really manage all the aspects to make sure they happen."*

Producer: *"Just out of curiosity, when your agent came out at renewal to go through your service plan and laid out when he would deliver policies, review claims, check your workers comp mod, review payroll, and set up a renewal strategy so you wouldn't waste your time or overpay for your insurance, were you comfortable with how they laid everything out?"*

Prospect: *"It's never been that formal a process."*

Producer: *"Well, maybe it's not that important because you've never had an unpaid claim or an extensive audit."*

Prospect: *"Wait a minute — this is important. If we had been doing this last year we wouldn't have had the surprise with..."*

Remember, selling involves playing the numbers while winning involves playing the probabilities. Using research to develop strategies for creating rapport, anticipating the prospect's problems, and creating clear, concrete images that highlight your strengths and the incumbent's weaknesses will set up your opportunity to **Drive The Wedge**.

I certainly hope that before you bought this book, you and your agency were doing some things right. I assume you have a few customers who think you've saved them time or money somewhere down the line. And I hope it wasn't all due to cut-throat pricing on your contracts. What are your best practices? Which things can you and your agency do just a little better or faster? What about you personally? It isn't good enough to say you'll go the extra mile. Describe the sights and attractions your customer will see along that mile. Get specific. And once you've done this introspective exercise, write it out on a sheet of paper or an index card, note it in your calendar, save it somewhere. One of the biggest favors you can do for yourself is to build a record of your best business practices.

Forget luck. Luck is for sellers, not winners. There is no substitution for preparation, research, and rehearsal. As a famous golf pro once said, "You know, the harder I work, the luckier I get."

Chapter Seven

Picture Perfect

There was a five-star General in a hospital. He was standing in front of a huge picture window. As he looked out on the idyllic scene before him—a beautiful mountain landscape, blue sky, and evergreen forests—he thinks to himself: "This is the most perfect scene I could imagine. This is picture perfect."

Why is the person in our little scene a five-star general? Because, like generals, prospects want to be in command. They're decision makers and don't like being pushed or pressured. The Wedge acknowledges this and is designed to keep the prospect in command at all times.

Similarly, commanding officers don't like to be told what they have done wrong, and neither do your prospects. The easiest way to get someone to be defensive is to begin attacking the decisions they have made. And yet, for many salespeople, this is standard operating procedure. When they see a problem, they go straight at the prospect with it, using phrases like "Did you know you're paying 50 percent more for this service?" or "The company you're working with has one of the worst reputations in the industry!"

And what happens? The prospect shuts down. He doesn't want to hear that he's an idiot, that his company has screwed up, that you are smarter than he is. Would you? Of course not. That's human nature.

The Wedge is a successful strategy for winning because it is based *entirely* on human nature. It works because it is easier to get someone to deny things are perfect than it is to admit there is a problem. Picture Perfect is a strategy creating conflict between the prospect and the incumbent by showing the prospect an ideal level of service. As the prospect compares his current level of service to his Picture Perfect vision, the difference he finds is the space into which you drive The Wedge.

You see, perfection is just a standard of service. And it is easier to get someone to say "No, the service I am getting does not meet *that* standard of excellence" than it is to get someone to say "Yes, I have a problem."

Creating Picture Perfect

The most important word in the concept of **Picture Perfect** is *picture*. The prospect must see, visualize, and have a clear image of the perfect level of service. To create that image, you need concrete words and descriptions that give him something solid to compare against the incumbent.

Giving your prospect the perfect picture requires that you create word pictures, in this case, the picture of ideal service. The key to creating word pictures is to use specific, concrete language, images that are low on the ladder of abstraction.

Think back to our examples in Chapter 5. Remember the guy who said his restaurant has good food. Well, what does "good" look like? What does it smell like?

If you ask the prospect to compare your good service, your customer-oriented approach, and your commitment to quality against the incumbent's, you will lose. You will lose because you're offering the same thing everyone else is. Every business has "good, customer-oriented, quality" service. Every agent is committed to excellence, everybody is using the same vague sales talk filled with empty words and no imagery.

This begs the question: Do you have a clear, concrete, and specific image of the service your company can provide? Can you create a word picture for a prospect that she can mentally hold up next to the incumbent?

If you can't define it, you will never be able to share it with the prospect, she will never be able to use it for comparison, and without that comparison, you look just like the incumbent. You lose.

The tough part of selling anything is that to be effective you have to be able to articulate the difference between what you offer the prospect and what the incumbent does. Unless you can create comparisons that show that one option is superior to another, you are just another seller wasting

Nothing is either good or bad except by comparison.

a prospect's time. The painful truth is that in most cases your competitors, including the incumbent, probably offer pretty much the same products and services that you do.

So how do you create differences? The winning difference is not in what you do, but rather how you do it. It's in the unique ways that you and your company deliver products and services that you can create favorable comparisons.

Therefore, the first step toward creating Picture Perfect is to consider what makes you different, the superior ways you provide the services your company offers. These differences can then be translated directly into benefits to the client.

Then, go through a process like the one on page 69, develop a clear, concrete, image-filled description of the ideal level of service. With this description, you create a picture of complete satisfaction and increased benefits for the prospect. When the prospect compares this ideal picture to his or her actual level of current service, the incumbent's performance will be inferior. Dissatisfaction equals pain and pain equals The Wedge.

The Winning Difference

Now let me answer a frequently asked question: "What if there aren't any major differences between what my agency offers and what my competitors do. In fact, I can't think of any one thing that we do so well that, when I tell the prospect about it, they'll be blown away. Sure, there are some little things I can do that add value — like put together a comprehensive safety plan for them and guarantee same-day responses to questions they have — but there's no one aspect of our service that will just knock their socks off."

And in most cases you're right. The reality is that there are three levels of difference:

1. Something that you do that is absolutely unique.
2. You have nothing unique, but have a better method of doing it. For example, anyone can cook a hamburger. It's how you cook it that can make it better, e.g., the right degree of doneness, heat level, seasonings used, and so on.
3. Your method isn't better than anyone else's. The difference is that you plan ahead and do it without prompting, not just on request.

Let's say that you are in a meeting with an insurance buyer and you're doing what a traditional agent would do. You'd tell them about your agency, how long you've been in business, which markets you represent, and that you have quality service. That's the usual approach. However, since almost every agent in America does exactly the same thing, the insurance buyer is left to make his decision on one factor alone: price.

So what would a Wedge producer do? By knowing and understanding the Three Levels of Differentiation he would do his research and identify the key processes or methods he uses that his competition doesn't that will keep the prospect ahead of the trouble curve. She would then develop her **Proactive Wedge** questions before entering the new business sales interview.

Here are some examples of things you might try to differentiate yourself from the incumbent:

- Provide a workers compensation modifier check sheet
- Review claims report for high reserves
- Assist in a payroll review to prevent an audit
- Update building values to prevent any coinsurance penalties
- Provide a business interruption worksheet to help prevent penalties

- Provide a coverage check sheet to help prevent any out-of-pocket claims

The next step in Picture Perfect is to present that perfect picture to the prospect in the right way.

"When you told your agent that..."

When the average salespeople of the world figure out that they can do something better than the incumbent, the farthest thing from their mind is assuming Picture Perfect. Instead, they inevitably attack their competitor (and, in the process, demean or question the judgment of the prospect). Here's an example:

> **Prospect:** *"Our agent doesn't seem to be consistent at getting out certificates on a timely basis."*

> **Salesperson:** *"You're not being treated fairly. We take pride in our ability to serve our customers. We have a 24-hour guarantee on certificates. In fact, we have a special computer in our office dedicated to producing certificates. And if you'll just call Sally, she'll get them out for you. That is what you want isn't it?"*

And another prospect shuts down rather than get berated by a salesperson.

The Wedge begins not with an attack on the incumbent or a fishing expedition of open-ended questions, but by assuming perfection already exists:

> **Prospect:** *"Our agent doesn't seem to be consistent at getting out certificates on a timely basis."*

> **Salesperson:** *"When you told your agent that you were unhappy with the fact that your certificates weren't getting out on time and that you wanted them to develop a method to get them out within twenty-four hours so you wouldn't have to worry about getting on job sites or getting your invoices paid, what did he say?"*

Note that there is no challenge to the prospect at all. Questions built on this model assume that the prospect is doing his job, that he has called his (incumbent) agent and is working on a solution to his company's problems.

There isn't any challenge to the incumbent either. Once again, you're assuming that the incumbent is providing Picture Perfect service. If he isn't, well, that's not your fault.

Why Picture Perfect Works

This approach works because there are three people in on every deal: the prospect, the incumbent, and the competitor. And built into every deal are potential points of conflict.

For example, consider the different views these people have on the issue of price. What is the prospect's price priority? He wants it as low as possible. What about the incumbent? He wants it to be as high as possible without losing the client.

What about service? The prospect always wants more service and more attention. The incumbent, being human, wants to do as little as possible. In other words, the incumbent wants to do the least amount of work required to keep his client.

This is true in every area of the incumbent's approach, and it might be true in your business life as well. Nobody likes to work any harder than necessary, that's human nature. But because the incumbent is only offering the necessary level of service as opposed to the *ideal* level of service, there is an opportunity to drive The Wedge.

The Wedge assumes that every party is doing what comes naturally: the prospect wants as much time, service, and attention as she can get, all at the lowest possible price, and the incumbent wants to spend as little time as possible on his client while collecting as much commission as he can.

More often than not, these are the prevailing conditions, which is why, more often than not, The Wedge works.

Chapter Eight

The Take Away

The Story thus far…

- You have shown the prospect the **Picture Perfect** level of service and performance.
- You have found the **Pain**, the problem or challenge that the prospect believes is truly important and feels strongly about addressing.

Your prospect has seen Picture Perfect—the level of service that he can imagine but does not have. His reaction is clear—he is not satisfied with what he has.

The question now is: How much does he care? Is he truly feeling *pain*? Is he ready to make a change?

To find out, we are going to show him another picture, the flip side of **Picture Perfect**: the **Take Away**. By dismissing the prospect's pain and taking away the benefits he would achieve by solving his problem, you will help the prospect see clearly what will be lost if he fails to act.

As a process, the Take Away is very simple: You state clearly the price of inaction and then dismiss it. As a technique, the Take Away is extremely effective.

How The Take Away Works

The prospect has told you that the incumbent is not doing the job, that there is distance between the service she is receiving and the service that is available. The prospect has either volunteered this information (a Reactive Wedge) or you have helped him discover it by using the Picture Perfect technique (a Proactive Wedge).

At this point, if Steve Sales were in the room, he would lunge right at the prospect with a pitch: "Boy, you must really be upset that you aren't getting the turn-around time you need. This must really be tough for you. If you were my client, I can assure you we would do a great job. Are you ready to get started?"

To which the answer is likely to be, "Naw, it's not that big a deal. We've got it under control. It's no biggie, really."

And you've just sold yourself out of a deal.

The Wedge is not about selling something. The Wedge works because it helps the prospect go through a process of self-discovery.

When you sat down with the prospect, he didn't know he was unhappy with his current service because he didn't have a true vision of how these services or products could be better. Using the Picture Perfect technique, he has discovered that he has a problem where he had not seen one before. It was always there. You didn't create it. You just helped him discover it.

The next step, the Take Away, allows the prospect to discover how important solving this problem truly is, how much it matters. An example:

You sell computer networking software and service, and you ask your prospect: "So, when your current service provider came out last month for his regular maintenance on your network server to anticipate your problems and keep your system from crashing; when he backed everything for you and scanned your hard drive to free up space and avoid losing service, were you satisfied with the results?

The prospect replies: "Actually, they only come out on service calls. We always back up our own data."

Take Away: "Oh, well, maybe it's not a big deal because networks never crash. And if it did, you just lose a day or two of productivity, right?

Now, if this prospect just had a client rip his head off last month because the server crashed and he wasn't able to provide the services he promised, his answer is going to be "Hell, yeah, it's a big deal. When our server crashes, my clients start climbing up my back!"

If you had announced that his computer crashes were horrifying disasters that put the future of the prospect's company at risk, he would have dismissed it as selling. And he would have been right. But by dismissing it for him, you force the prospect to think about how important this problem truly is. He has to commit, intellectually, to the importance of solving the problem at hand.

There are a million Take Aways, one for every benefit you and your product or service can provide. However, the format is almost always the same (See page 29).

You always begin with The Wedge subject, the specific improvement in products or services that you have presented to the prospect. You then dismiss it as unimportant, as "no big deal," or "not a significant problem," followed by the word "because."

The *because* phrase is a clear statement of benefits lost, dismissed as an unimportant consequence: "because your company is so big, it can afford to spend a little extra every month," or "because your clients are probably so loyal they don't really mind if they have to wait on delivery of your products," etc., etc.

If your Take Away is accurate, and the issue is not particularly important to the prospect, he will let it go by. By doing so, the prospect is letting you know that you need to move on to another Wedge issue and another concern.

But if you have found true pain in the prospect, if you have raised an issue that would be important enough to consider firing the incumbent over, the prospect will not allow it to be dismissed. Instead of resisting your suggestions of a need to change, he will assert his own belief that change may be in order.

Why The Take Away Works

The Take Away is based on a rather primitive notion called the Boy/Girl Theory, which says that what you got you don't want, and what you ain't got, you're always lusting after.

Not sophisticated, perhaps, but true.

The lesson of Boy/Girl theory is not that you should play hard to get, but that pushing someone to do something almost always creates resistance, no matter how beneficial the action you are pushing may be. Prospects are people, they aren't computers. If they feel put off, if they sense that they are being pressured, the emotional response is enough to kill the deal.

The Take Away is a 180-degree approach. Instead of pushing someone to agree that it's time to make a change, you are pushing her to defend the benefits of change. When you say "You absolutely must....," the natural human reaction is "No, I don't," and to shut the discussion down.

But when you say "Don't bother doing..., it's not that important," the natural human reaction is to say "Now wait a minute. Doing...might be the best thing for me and my company. Let's talk about it."

If this all seems like a game to you...hey, you might be right. That's why we talk about Game Theory earlier in this book. But this is a game that only works when the prospect is truly moving forward in the process of self-discovery.

The Take Away technique is vital if your prospect is going to discover for herself the need for change. Every day, prospects are intellectualizing problems and challenges their businesses face but either cannot or do not solve. ***Remember:*** if you sell the need for change, the customer is almost always willing to push right back, to say it's no big deal, to continue to deny the legitimate needs you have identified.

So they don't increase their insurance coverage or they don't advertise enough or they don't get the additional software support they need and, one day, what happens? They get stung.

But when they do get stung—not enough insurance coverage, their production costs are too high, their computer infrastructure fails them—whose fault is it? No, it's not the incumbent's fault, it's not the prospect's fault. It is YOUR fault. You didn't do your job, you let them off the hook and, if what you sell really is worthwhile, they have missed a true opportunity and will eventually pay the price.

Let me give you an example that is close to home for most of us:

Most of us have families. We have husbands, wives, and children who depend on us. We know that we should be preparing for the future, we know that Social Security won't provide all of the financial support we are going to need when we get older. But we justify our failure to act by pushing back that timeline, by rationalizing our failure to save, invest, or prepare for the inevitable.

Down deep inside, in our latent memories, we know we need to act. But we justify our inaction and ignore our problem.

Then a salesman knocks on our door and points out that legitimate need. And what do we do? We convince this so-called high pressure salesman that we will figure it out one day, so we don't need his insurance or his investment product or his savings plan. And you know what: that salesperson is a failure. He didn't fail because he didn't make a sale. He failed because he let us down. We needed to act, and he didn't do his job and create within us the vision to do so.

I know this first hand. My father is in his mid-70s. And somewhere out there is a stupid life insurance salesman who let him off the hook. He could have made the payments, he could have begun an investment program, he could have put a plan in action.

If he had done what was best for my dad instead of what was easier for him, my dad would have bought it. And it would have been the best thing for his life.

But he didn't. My father didn't see clearly the benefits of acting or the costs of inaction, all he could see was the few dollars each month in premiums. And he is paying the price today.

Whose fault is it? Of course, my father has to take responsibility, but he is also suffering the consequences. The person I blame is that lazy, incompetent life insurance salesman out there who didn't have the guts to get my father to see the vision he needed to make a change, to act.

The Challenge Of The Take Away

In my years of sales training, I have found that the Take Away is one of the most difficult concepts for sales people to master. Why?

Part of the reason is that the Take Away is so counter-intuitive. In the Take Away, you are generally saying the opposite of what you really mean. Your words may be saying "Oh, it's no big deal…" but your tone and demeanor are screaming: "What are you, crazy? You've got to do something about this problem!"

As such, Take Aways are incongruent messages, and the tension gets people's attention. Psychologically, they throw people off balance. It takes a little getting used to, but it is a powerful technique.

Another reason producers tend to have problems with the Take Away is because many salespeople don't want the responsibility that comes from truly being able to make a difference in the lives of others.

For a salesperson who claims to believe in the products he sells and the company he represents, The Wedge can be very dangerous. For if the things you are telling your prospects are true, then you have a duty, a burden to help them discover the benefit that is available to them and to help them take action now.

The producers I work with have realized: "Hey, if I see the legitimate problems facing the prospect but I can't find a way to get her to see it, too, then it is MY fault." By failing to sell, you aren't just letting your company down. You are letting the prospect down.

I don't care what you sell, how tangible or intangible the product or service may be. If you can provide your products or services in a way that will honestly benefit your clients, you need to find a way to get them to see it. I don't care if you sell insurance, intellectual property, or industrial toilet paper—if you can really help people and their businesses prosper, you have a duty to show them how.

Because if you can help a business owner save enough money on paper products each year to pay his daughter's university tuition, you aren't selling toilet paper—you are making someone's life better.

Chapter Nine

Vision Box and Replay

Up to this point:

- You have shown the prospect the **Picture Perfect** level of service and performance.
- You have found the **Pain**, the problem or challenge that the prospect believes is truly important and feels strongly about addressing.
- Using the **Take Away** you have helped the prospect articulate clearly that solving this problem is important to him, committing himself emotionally and intellectually to a solution.

For some of the more entrenched sellers, the **Vision Box** is the most difficult technique to master because it requires the producer to do something completely out of character: *Let someone else talk.*

But for those producers well-schooled in the open-ended question approach, the Vision Box will be your opportunity to shine. You will need your questioning skills, too, because this isn't a bull session we're talking about. As in every step of The Wedge, you have a very specific task in mind.

The task is to get a Vision Box statement from the prospect that is as clear, concrete and visual as the Picture Perfect you gave her earlier. If you can do that you will have achieved your goal. But it won't be easy.

The Vision Box at Work

Thanks to the Take Away, the prospect has made the emotional commitment to change. She has seen the level of service she wants and has said that achieving it is important. But so far, you've done most of the talking. The prospect has seen *your* vision of the future. Now it's time for you to see hers.

If you used the rapport techniques discussed earlier and created an environment of comfort and credibility, then getting the prospect to talk won't be the problem. Getting her to tell you what she wants, that's the problem.

You see, prospects have the same problems communicating that salespeople do. They want "better quality," they're "committed to excellence," and they have "long-term strategies for growth."

The prospect has seen the benefits of change. He honestly believes you can help him get where he wants to go, only he can't tell you where that is. Like the salespeople from Chapter 5 who were stuck way up on the ladder of abstraction, the prospect will tell you he wants to go "north," when he really wants to go to the corner of Main and Elm in downtown Milwaukee, Wisconsin.

So the challenge is to ask questions that will encourage the prospect to fill out the Vision Box — in your mind and in hers — with a clear, colorful, concrete image of the services she wants, the problems she would like to solve, and the new way she would like to do business.

How do you do this? By using outstanding communication skills, along with intelligent, planned and well-rehearsed questioning to help the prospect fill in the concrete details of abstract concepts like "grow" or "dominate our market" or "finally get consistent and significant savings over the long-term."

"So, what would you like to have happen?"

The first essential question will be, "How would you like this [the specific area of the prospect's business where you have found the pain] to work? What would you like to see happen?" This question is likely to elicit a vague answer, no matter how specifically you ask, so use follow-up questions to help the prospect define his terms, set specific goals, and detail the solutions to problems of the past which have left him dissatisfied.

The key thing to remember about the Vision Box is that you can be almost certain that the prospect doesn't know what he wants to begin with. He may know he's dissatisfied, and he may want "better service" or "more hands-on support," but those comments are so high up the infamous ladder of abstraction that they are essentially useless.

The producer's job at this point is to help the prospect down the ladder until the description of his vision of ideal service is so clear that you can repeat it back to him. Intelligent, directed questioning can help.

Pertinent questions include: When you say "_____" what do you mean? You've mentioned growth: do you have some specific goals? When you say you want "_____", how would that work? What, specifically, would you like to change?

The key is to elicit specifics, i.e., concrete language and images. If the prospect says "I would like to get my reports faster," your question should be: "How fast? What do you really need?" If she says she wants regular meetings with the agent, find out if regular means once a day or once a quarter.

This process is called the Vision Box for a reason. Until the prospect has a clear, concrete, describable vision of what she actually wants, you won't know what she wants from you. **Remember:** chances are the incumbent offers the same products and services you do. He just hasn't taken advantage of the opportunity to find out what is truly important to the client, how he can truly help the client succeed.

When you have a clear vision of the goals and aspirations of the client and a real, workable approach to help him achieve these goals — when you have all this and the incumbent doesn't — you've made progress, but you haven't won yet.

The Replay

The next step is to make sure that you understand the client's desires and objectives by repeating them back to him or her, clearly and concretely. This is the Replay.

There isn't much more to be said about The Replay other than one final, very important point that applies to both The Replay and The Vision Box. During these two steps, your greatest temptation and worst enemy will be to use the words "me" and "I." *Avoid them at all costs.*

During the Vision Box and Replay parts of a sales call, I like to think of myself as an architect who has a friend planning to build a house. Because he is a friend, and I'm in the building business, I'm interested in his plans and excited about seeing his vision fulfilled. I'm not, however, trying to sell my services as the contractor.

We talk about windows, landscaping, the latest household gadgets and building techniques as my friend tries to get me to envision his dream house, and I try to ask specific questions that make that vision clearer for both of us.

As long as we're talking about how my friend wants to get somebody in to put down a masonry floor or custom design a walk-in closet, the conversation is both honest and enthusiastic.

But what happens as soon as I say, "Buddy, let me build this house for you. I'll give you a good price." Suddenly, we're negotiating instead of communicating. He stops telling me what he really wants and starts telling me what he thinks he can afford. I become a seller, and he becomes a buyer.

Somehow, we want the conversation to transition naturally from the prospect talking about *somebody* to the prospect asking "how can *you* help me?" You want this to happen because the prospect has asked, not because you have suggested.

The temptation is to say "Let me do this" or "Our company offers everything you need." Don't do it. Don't start selling because, as soon as you start with "I can do this," or "Let me take care of..." the prospect feels it and begins shutting down. He or she starts thinking: "If I'm not careful, somebody is going to be asking me for a check. I'd better shut up."

Don't tell, ask. Don't talk, listen. Once you have the clear vision, lay it out so that she can see you have it and will conclude you can help her achieve it.

You want to help the prospect create a mental bridge between points A and B, with the building materials provided by you. When the prospect sees you as the bridge between where he is and the benefits of where he could be, he will ask you. And when you're being asked, you have all the power.

Chapter Ten

Raising the White Flag

The Story so far:

- You've shown the prospect the **Picture Perfect** level of service and performance.
- You've found the **Pain**, the problem or challenge that the prospect believes is truly important and feels strongly about addressing.
- Using the **Take Away**, you've helped the prospect clearly articulate that solving this problem is important to her, committing emotionally and intellectually to a solution.
- You've heard the prospect's vision of the level of service he would like to receive, and you gave him a **Replay** of that vision by going back over it with him.

If you've successfully followed the first five steps of the Wedge, when you get to the final step—**The White Flag**—the prospect will appear so ready to buy that every fiber in your body will be tingling with the desire to "sell, sell, sell!" Don't do it.

Remember, you aren't in the *selling* business anymore. The Wedge gets you out of the selling business and into the closing business, the *winning* business. The average salesperson wants to go on the attack, throwing sales babble at the prospect and sticking contracts under people's noses. That's selling, and it doesn't work.

I know what you're thinking: "Randy, you're out of your mind! I've got this guy! He's beggin' me to sell. I can feel it! Let me sell!"

That's the temptation. The Wedge has helped the prospect discover for himself that he wants and needs to make a change, and you want to pitch yourself and your company as the solution. It makes sense. It is exactly what a seller would do—ask the prospect to buy.

But winners know that the strongest position to be in is for the prospect to *ask you* to sell.

Sellers spend their time asking prospects to buy…and being rejected. When you are out pushing yourself and your product, everything is working against you. You are on the wrong side of the Boy/Girl Theory. The laws of physics, particularly inertia, are aligned against you. Not surprisingly, when you *sell*, you don't often close. Using The Wedge means taking the opposite approach so, when done properly, instead of pushing the prospect to buy, you're pushed by the prospect to sell.

In the last chapter, we used the example of an architect listening to a friend's plans to build a house. Let's return to that for a minute. If the architect has been a true friend, helping his pal visualize the picture perfect home and showing him how to achieve it, the perfectly natural conclusion of that conversation is for the architect's friend to ask him: "Can you help me build this dream house?"

At the same time, it would be very unnatural, and rather annoying, for the architect to ask his friend for a check. Friends don't ask friends to submit bids.

If you can create the natural dynamic between you and the prospect of two friends working together to achieve a goal, you have created the best possible opportunity to close. Everything that was working against the seller is working for you as the friend being asked to step in and help.

Falling on the Sword

The sixth and final step is not for you to assault the prospect's business "fortress," but to raise a White Flag that makes the prospect feel comfortable lowering the drawbridge and inviting you in. The example I use to illustrate this is *The Sword*.

Too many producers, instead of raising the White Flag, act as if they are wielding a sword, slashing and attacking others, spreading fear and dread wherever they go. They see their sales pitch as a weapon they use to force reluctant prospects to capitulate. These people don't want to join the prospect's team, they want the would-be customer to yield before their superior sales firepower.

You can see it in their presentations: They line up their statistics like cannons on a ridge. They target the prospect's weaknesses ("I can beat the price he's getting," or "I'm gonna stomp all over his current turn-around time"). They prepare for battle, put on their lucky three-piece suit and, at the first sign of prospect pain, they unsheathe their sales sword and start slashing away! Not surprisingly, these salespeople are rarely greeted with open arms by their prospects.

If you must view your services and benefits as a sword, that's OK. However, we don't want to use the sword to defeat the prospect/incumbent relationship by force. We want to keep the sword sheathed, and instead raise the White Flag, so that the prospect invites us in.

For the prospect, it's the difference between being attacked and overcome by the producer — never a pleasant experience—or realizing for herself that she needs to make a change and willingly choosing to do so.

How the White Flag Works

The prospect is sitting across from you, convinced that it's time for a change, that there is both a problem and, he hopes, a solution. But he has yet to take a single action committing himself to that change.

At this point in the process, the primary obstacle to closing isn't the prospect. It's you and your desire to rush forward and seize the deal for yourself. "Let me tell you how my company can make the changes you need" is a sentence that resides on the tip of every seller's tongue.

But you aren't going to do that. Instead, you are going to conclude the Replay of the prospect's vision of how he would like his problems solved by asking the question: "So, what would you like me to do?" The prospect isn't under assault. He is in control.

If you have established rapport and helped the prospect discover the kind of true pain that can drive The Wedge deeply, his response to your question will be to invite you in immediately.

Ideally, the prospect will affirmatively indicate that she is prepared to act. You will hear statements that begin with questions like "Can you really help me..." or "I'm ready to go," or "Will you..."

And, of course, you will oblige. But before you tell her that, you need to resume the prospect's journey of self-discovery because the second obstacle that might prevent her from buying is her inability to see that her problem is the incumbent.

Your job is to get the prospect to see that the specific business problems facing him (the pain that has driven The Wedge) are just symptoms. The prospect must see that the only way to cure these symptoms — higher costs, slow turnaround time, ongoing technical problems —- is to deal with the real problem, the incumbent agent or company. *They* are the reason why the prospect is dissatisfied and he must see that clearly before he will be ready to act.

By saying to you "Can you lower my price" or "can you put an end to all the technical glitches," the prospect is saying, in effect, anyone who can solve these problems is the solution — including the incumbent. And, of course, if the incumbent gets the chance, he will promise to make everything right too. Most likely he will try to use his relationship with the prospect to keep you blocked out.

So, when the prospect asks for your help, the answer isn't "Sure! Let me bring in a proposal next week!" If you give her that answer, she will spend the week being sweet-talked by the incumbent. And why not? After all, the prospect figures that the agent (incumbent) isn't the problem, the unsatisfactory service is.

If you don't leave the prospect with the belief that the unsatisfactory service is a result of inattentiveness and inability, you've failed. For soon after you leave with an opportunity to quote in your pocket, the prospect's old pal the incumbent is going to show up with a bottle of scotch and a couple of glasses. He's going to sit down across from your prospect and remind him about the lunches they've shared and the gifts they exchanged during the holidays. He's going to confess to his failings, promise to fix every problem you've identified and make every prospect's dream come true. If necessary, he'll tell the prospect in a quivering voice about lil' "Incumbent Jr." who's in college and how much his Daddy needs this account to pay the tuition.

In short, the incumbent is going to make it as hard as possible for the prospect to make a change. Change is painful and, if the incumbent has anything to say about it, it will be more painful to change than to do nothing, even if the service isn't all it could be.

Suddenly you've gone from a prospect who is practically begging you to sell, to a prospect who won't take your calls. Congratulations! You've just been rolled.

The prospect must see that the incumbent is the problem, that what he is asking you to do is to help him fire the incumbent and not just fix the symptoms. He needs to see precisely what is involved in making the change from the incumbent to you. To do this, we use the *Rehearsal* technique.

Here's the Rehearsal at work:

Prospect: *"I'd like for you to give me a proposal on how you can help me achieve these goals?"*

Salesperson: *"Well, I'd be happy to. But it's going to create a real problem for you."*

Prospect: *"What kind of problem?"*

Salesperson: *"Suppose for a moment that it's three weeks from now, you're looking at my proposal and it has everything you've asked for. The three key elements we just went over are all in there and you are* *confident that it will make the difference for you and your firm. Can you imagine that?"*

Prospect: *"OK, I can imagine that."*

Salesperson: *"As you look at the proposal and say to yourself 'I think I've found a new agent,' that creates a dilemma. I'm wondering, can we deal with that?"*

Prospect: *"What's the dilemma?"*

Salesperson: *"The problem is when you decide that you want to make this change, how are you going to tell your current agent that it's over?"*

Prospect: *"Hmmm, I never thought about it…"*

And now, ladies and gentlemen, we are at the crux of the matter. Recall the challenge from the beginning of this book. Why do we need The Wedge? Because until the prospect is ready to fire the incumbent, you don't have a prospect!

The White Flag is the moment that the prospect realizes this and prepares, in his mind, to fire the incumbent. If he will not fire the incumbent, you won't close. Our entire strategy is to get the prospect to see the benefits of change, to feel the need for change, to have a clear, concrete vision of a brighter future. But it won't work if the prospect can't go through the pragmatic steps of actually making the change, which means firing the incumbent.

The Rehearsal technique takes the prospect into that future moment when he is going to fire the incumbent, show the prospect how difficult it is going to be, and take him through a rehearsal of how to get it done.

Let's return to our dialog:

Prospect: *"Hmmm, I never thought about it…"*

Salesperson: *"Well, can I tell you what's going to happen when your agent finds out you are making a change: He'll rush right over and say everything he can think of to keep you right where you are right now. When he does, how are you going to handle that?"*

Prospect: *"Well, I'll just have to explain to him that business is business."*

Salesperson: *"Can you do it?"*

Prospect: *"Sure…"*

Salesperson: *"And when he comes in the employee entrance with a wine and cheese basket, pours you a glass of the good stuff and says 'You can't do this to me!' how are you going to handle it?"*

Prospect: *"You think he'll really do that?"*

Salesperson: *"He will do anything he can think of to hang onto your account. When he shows up, how are you going to handle that?"*

Prospect: *"I'm ready to make a change, and I will explain that fact to my current agent."*

Salesperson: *"Can you do it?"*

Prospect: *"Absolutely. Not a problem."*

Salesperson: *"Then I'll get started on your proposal right away…"*

And the deal is closed.

By asking a series of questions such as "How are you going to handle that?" and "Can you do it?," you continue to focus the prospect on the difficult task he faces in the future. Keep doing this until you are satisfied that the prospect is prepared to fire the incumbent. You will have to rely on your intuition to some degree, but at some point you will become confident that the prospect is ready to act. When he's ready, so are you.

Why Rehearse?

When dealing with a prospect involved in an unsatisfactory incumbent relationship you face an interesting dilemma: The prospect's heart and mind are in the wrong place.

97

If the prospect is unsatisfied with the service he's getting from the incumbent, why hasn't he made a change? Because he is rationalizing his pain. He has either decided that there is no such thing as perfect service and that this is the best he can get, that his problem isn't important enough to worry about, or he has pushed it out of his mind and intends to deal with it later. His pain is real, but he has rationalized his way out of dealing with it.

Meanwhile, while he is rationalizing his legitimate disappointment or concern and has emotionalized the relationship he has with the incumbent. He doesn't want his agent, who he knows, to feel bad. "Hey, nobody's perfect" is the defense mechanism of a customer who knows that he's not totally satisfied with his agent's performance but doesn't want the emotional stress of making a change.

The Rehearsal technique is a valuable way to deal with this problem. It works by walking the prospect through the emotional experience of an unpleasant task — firing someone — so that she can deal with it on a purely intellectual level when the time comes.

Therapists often use this technique. They use it to prepare people in counseling for a future event, removing the emotional edge of their client's likely response and helping her react intellectually. They will tell clients things like "When you go home, your husband is going to. . . How will you react? How do you want to react?"

These questions don't displace or deny emotions. Instead, they bring the emotions out, allowing for a release. When the counselor says "Your husband is going to tell you . . .," the subject feels the emotions rising and can deal with them in a Rehearsal setting. Nothing's on the line, and there is a very friendly audience.

If this seems a little too much like social work, think about how often you see these situations every day. You're in the office and you see a fellow employee is really annoyed about something. You walk into her office and say, "Hey, how's it going?" She unloads on you about how the manager took away a project or didn't give her the schedule she had been promised. The point is, when she is done with the legitimate emotional reaction (i.e., venting), she is in a much better frame of mind to confront the manager and deal with the issues at hand.

By talking through the problem with you, and letting off emotional steam, she is now ready to take care of the matter in a more thoughtful, controlled way. But until she resolved the emotional conflict, she was not prepared.

Your prospects are the same way. If the issue were just "do you like me, the salesman, and want to hire me?," we would all be closing 90 percent of the time. But there is an incumbent out there, and we can't close the deal until both the prospect and the incumbent have dealt with the oncoming change.

Chapter Eleven

Finding Your Winning Wedge Every Time

The Story thus far...

1. You have shown the prospect the **Picture Perfect** level of service and performance.
2. You have found the pain, the problem or challenge that the prospect believes is truly important and feels strongly about addressing.
3. Using the **Take Away**, you have helped the prospect articulate clearly that solving this problem is important to him, committing himself emotionally and intellectually to a solution.
4. You have heard the prospect's **Vision** of the level of service he would like to receive, and you gave him a **Replay** of that vision by going back over it with him.
5. Because you "raised the **White Flag**" instead of selling, the prospect has invited you in, literally asking you to sell to him.
6. You point out that selling to him will create a dilemma: What about the incumbent? Using the **Rehearsal** technique, you help the prospect realize that, to achieve his goals, the prospect must fire the incumbent.

You close the deal...and **Win!**

These are the six steps of The Wedge and, if I were a typical salesperson, I would tell you that "They are guaranteed to work... every time!" But the entire philosophy of The Wedge is to develop an honest strategy to deal with the real problems preventing you from closing, and I'm not going to start lying to you now.

So let me tell you right now: The Wedge doesn't *always* work.

Sometimes you'll know five minutes into the meeting that no matter what you do, this prospect will find a way to kill the deal. Other times, you won't be able to find any pain. The prospect is going to beam with satisfaction at his incumbent's service. Then there will always be those people who just don't believe anything a salesman says, who won't see a dime's worth of difference between you and every other salesperson in the world, no matter what you say or do.

That's reality. But while The Wedge doesn't guarantee success, it does drastically increase your odds by giving you a winning strategy before you even begin your meeting. The six steps of The Wedge that we've covered will have an immediate impact on your business. You will close more; you will win more.

Of course there's no such thing as a sure thing and you are going to run into situations like the ones mentioned below. Don't panic. There are some additional strategies that you can use to increase your chances to close these deals, too.

Broken Deal #1:
The Prospect Isn't Convinced
You Can Get the Job Done

You've gotten the prospect to talk about the pain he's having with his service from the incumbent. He's told you his Vision for the level of service he would like to have and you've done a Replay showing that you understand clearly. But when you ask: "OK, what would you like for me to do?," his answer is "Well, what *can* you do?"

The prospect knows he could use some help. He's just not convinced that you can help him. And, quite frankly, why should he be?

We live in an era of heightened cynicism. Your prospects have sales hacks barging through their door every day, making promises and throwing around charts, graphs and guarantees. If the prospect is a good business person, he already knows the service he's receiving isn't the best. He has probably tried to solve the problem once or twice already. He may have concluded that what he's got is the industry standard, that satisfactory service just isn't available.

What you need for Doubting Thomas' like this is a plan to help them convince themselves that you and your company can deliver. No, that doesn't mean "selling" with a new set of handouts and five more pages of statistics. That's not strategy, that's just a heavier dose of the same old snake oil.

The **Convincer Strategy** works because it acknowledges that you can't actually *convince* anyone of anything. People must discover the truth for themselves.

There are five basic ways people get information to convince themselves that something is true: their own senses of sight, hearing, touch, taste, and smell. Set aside the last two and we can build a strategy that allows doubting prospects to see, hear, or feel what they must to convince themselves they can move forward with you.

When the prospect's doubt appears, you want to offer a solution that will meet his or her criteria for certainty. When the prospect says, "Can you help me?," you want to let him know that you are aware of the problem. Here's an example:

Salesperson: *"So, what would you like for me to do?"*

Prospect: *"I don't know. What can you do?"*

Salesperson: *"We can fix this problem, we're the best at it...but you expect me to say that, don't you? Because you still see me as just another salesperson."*

Prospect: *"Sure, I guess."*

Salesperson: *"So how do you know that when I tell you we can get it done that I'm telling you the truth? Do you need to see a plan of action?*

Do you need to see letters of reference? Do you want to talk to some people I've worked with and let them tell you themselves? Or do you go with your gut feeling? How would you know?"

You have just offered the prospect a menu of Convincer options from which he can choose. You give him the opportunity to come back in one of those primary modes. And, because you are working the Wedge, you have a strategy for each answer.

For example, if he says he wants to see the reports ("I gotta see the numbers for myself before I can make a decision") here is your response:

Salesperson: *"Let's say I come back with three or four letters from people you know, the reports, the documentation, all the numbers, everything you need to see. What happens next?"*

Prospect: *"You do that, and I'll ask you to [give me a proposal, bid, etc]."*

Salesperson: *"When you do, that is going to create a new dilemma. I wonder if we can talk about that...."*

You are now in the **Rehearsal** technique outlined in the previous chapter. The same technique works if the prospect wants to talk to your references:

Salesperson: *"You say you like to talk to people. How many people would you like to talk to?"*

Prospect: *"Oh, two or three. Maybe four."*

Salesperson: *"If I give you those names, will you call them?"*

Prospect: *"Sure."*

Salesperson: *"Can I count on that?"*

Prospect: *"Yes, you can."*

Salesperson: *"OK, let's suppose you speak to them and they tell you that we are real, that we can do what we say we can do. What happens next?"*

Prospect: *"If they do that, I'll ask you to [give me a proposal, bid, etc]."*

Salesperson: *"And that's going to create a dilemma for you…"*

And we're back in the **Rehearsal.**

If they're like a lot of the old-style business people who work off instinct, there isn't as much room for strategy. If I have a prospect who is clearly dubious about my ability to deliver what we both know he wants, and they tell me they are the "go with the gut" type, I usually just ask, "Well, how am I doing?"

In a surprising number of instances, that question alone resolves the doubt. I usually get a response like "You're doin' fine," or "I'm with you," something along those lines. By asking the question, you will demonstrate that you are listening, that you understand the problem and the need to solve it.

The Convincer strategy is a proven, workable technique that can turn an entire deal around. It works on the premise that the customer cares more about his business than you do (a realistic assumption) and wants it to grow and prosper. He wants solutions. It also acknowledges all of the damage that has been done to business relationships by "sellers."

Broken Deal #2:
The Happy Camper

Believe it or not, some agents really are providing terrific service for their clients. They're getting the job done and, no matter how many Wedges we drive, they are not going to find their agent or his performance unsatisfactory. There is no pain to exploit. And you know what we say: "No pain, no change."

Well, don't give up...yet. There is still a strategy for you to pursue that will keep you in the hunt, "The Best Deal Close." It works something like this:

You've tried several proactive Wedges, but you haven't found any pain. The prospect tells you that everything is great. So you drop your head down, shake your head, whatever it takes to communicate an internal dilemma — "Can I tell you about the problem I have?" You give a big sigh and say:

Producer: *"Here's my problem. I've got this [carrier, situation, price, deal] that is giving me the opportunity to come in at a really great price. Lately we've been blowing other people away. Problem is, when I started giving people this price, the competition got wind of it and got a chance to minimize the difference. They can't match it, but they've ended up keeping the business and I ended up getting used.*

I'm curious, in order to keep that from happening, what would have to happen for you to be willing to compare my best deal and your agent's best deal and let the best deal win? No second looks, no going back to [the carrier, the underwriter, etc], no behind the back dunks. Just my best deal against his best deal and let the best deal win."

Prospect: *"Sure, I'll do it."*

What the prospect has just done is let you know that the relationship with the incumbent is breakable. If he says "No way, I always give my guy another chance," or if he won't give you an answer, then you probably cannot break up the incumbent relationship and you should leave your card, thank him for the coffee, and go to your next appointment.

However, if he opens the door at all, you know you have a chance. It could be possible that the incumbent is providing fine service but that there is no real relationship. If you can match the incumbent, you might win. Whatever the motivation, the Best Deal Close can keep you in the game.

It keeps you in the game by getting you back to the **Rehearsal**. In the previous example, you would immediately go to "OK, let's say we come back and my deal beats his. This creates a dilemma for you..." and you are back walking him through the firing of the incumbent.

There is another answer to the Best Deal Close that I've often heard:

> **Producer:** *"What would have to happen for you to consider his best deal and my best deal and let the best deal win?"*
>
> **Prospect:** *"I don't know, I mean, he's been our agent for quite a while, and that wouldn't be fair. We're loyal to people like that. You'd have to beat his price by a pretty big margin."*
>
> **Producer:** *"How much?"*
>
> **Prospect:** *"Oh, at least 20-25 percent..."*

Once again, the prospect has told you the deal is breakable. He calls it being "loyal." If the relationship is breakable, you have a reason to stay in the fight.

> **Producer:** *"So, let's suppose it's six weeks from now and there is my deal and its 20 percent less, what happens next?"*
>
> **Prospect:** *"You beat his price by 20 percent and the deal is yours."*
>
> **Producer:** *"20 percent, you're comfortable with that?"*
>
> **Prospect:** *"Sure."*
>
> **Producer:** *"OK, can we deal with the real problem? Suppose I come back with my deal and it's 20 percent less, how are you going to tell the other guy it's over? You know he's gonna cry and put a lot of pressure on you to stay"*

And you're back at **Rehearsal**, which you take all the way to the close.

> **Salesperson:** *"So, are you prepared to tell him you've made this change?"*
>
> **Prospect:** *"Yes, I'm comfortable with that."*

[Now, we add a new twist]

Salesperson: *"OK, can I tell you my problem? I can't do 20 percent. No way, it's just not possible. I can probably do 10%, maybe a little better, but not 20 percent. I realize that's probably not enough. So what do you want me to do, leave?*

Prospect: *"I don't know. I mean, you said 20 percent"*

Salesperson: *I know I can beat his price by 10 percent and if you do $100,000, that's an extra ten grand you're spending right there. I suppose having your current agent is worth an extra $10,000 to you."*

This is truly the end of the line. What you've done is force the prospect to quantify the value of the incumbent relationship. Few relationships can withstand this sort of scrutiny. If the incumbent does, he deserves to keep the client. If not, you've created a Wedge on the issue of price.

The **Best Deal Close** is not the best way to close a deal. In fact, it's one of the worst. But in cases where there is no pain to exploit, it can create a last-chance opportunity to close.

Broken Deal #3:
The Shallow Wedge

Sometimes, even the most experienced salesperson just can't find any pain. You may have identified a problem the prospect would like to solve, but not one that he perceives as important enough to justify the pain of make a change. Without the emotional force of true pain, The Wedge has "glanced off," and you are not in a position to close.

What do you do? Go back and look again. Use a Proactive Wedge to raise an issue you haven't discussed before. If that doesn't work, use another. As long as the rapport is there and you have Proactive Wedges to drive, keep going. If there was enough discontent there to keep you moving forward the first time, chances are the pain exists. You just need to keep looking for its true source.

This is why it's important to always have several Proactive Wedges prepared before you go into any sales call. Sellers have to rely on their one pitch and hope it works. Not you. You've prepared, you've rehearsed, and you are going to create opportunity after opportunity to have a legitimate shot at winning.

Broken Deal #4: The Bad Feeling

The one thing that I hope this book has proven to you beyond any doubt is that most of our success is driven by emotion. If you connect with a prospect, if you can establish rapport, if you can help her see the possibility of achieving for her business what she hopes to achieve, you can establish a powerful emotional bond in a matter of minutes.

At the same time, it is possible to have the opposite reaction with a prospect. She looks at you and you look at her and wham! Loathing at first sight. Modeling and mirroring won't help. The chemistry is wrong, and nothing will go right.

What do you do?

If you feel it, say it. If you feel that the meeting just isn't working, let the prospect know that you know it, too. The worst thing that can happen is that you save yourself and the prospect a few wasted minutes. And it's always possible that acknowledging an awkward situation will break the ice and give you another opportunity to connect.

You just look at the prospect and say: "I sense that this is not working. Is that a fair statement?" It's a gutsy strategy, to be sure, but once again, we're trying to create a climate for truth-telling. Being that direct has the potential to create deal-breaking levels of confrontation, but dishonesty isn't going to create opportunity, anyway.

Up or out should be your approach. Either you and your prospect are going to move upward toward mutual understanding and communication, or you should get out of his office and go to another appointment.

Conclusion

This chapter could be an entire book in itself, because the number of things that can go wrong in a prospect meeting are as varied and unpredictable as the prospects themselves. The prospects aren't going to quote directly out of these sample scripts anymore than you are.

However, the principles are always the same. The prospect's concerns and motivations will be the same. And you will be prepared to address every obstacle, dodge, and strategy of the prospect's game — no matter how unexpected or unusual — if you will commit yourself to these strategies:

- Know what your prospect's concerns and problems are likely to be so you can anticipate them.
- Establish rapport so that you can help your prospect on his journey of self-discovery regarding his business and his relationship with the incumbent.
- Identify pain, which is the source of the energy you need to break the incumbent relationship.
- Concretely demonstrate how you and your firm can deliver the goods and services the prospect needs in a way that will resolve that pain and satisfy her goals for her company.
- Tell the truth.
- Connect personally with the prospect.
- Paint perfect pictures of service for the prospect to compare with the incumbent's real level of service.
- Never offer to act, always position yourself to be invited to act.

- Force the prospect to clearly state what he truly wants to accomplish.
- Repeat your understanding of the prospect's desires back to him, and listen carefully to his response.
- Never forget that the prospect's problem is not the unsatisfactory product or service, it is the incumbent agent who is providing that product or service.
- Never forget your Number One obstacle in every deal is the incumbent.

Master these techniques, learn these principles, and you will be able to enter every meeting with a prospective client knowing that you will have a legitimate opportunity to close. More importantly, you will leave every meeting knowing that you explored every opportunity to close, no matter the result.

When you can conclude every business day with these confidences, you'll no longer be selling, *you'll be winning*.

Appendix

"The Wedge" is a tool. Like any other tool, you have to practice with it.

In this appendix, we have provided you with several tools to help you write and develop your own Proactive and Reactive Wedges. In addition, there are scripting tools for the Rehearsal, Convincer Strategy, and Best Deal Close.

Write your own scripts and practice them on your sales team first. Then for a free evaluation of your "Wedge" scripts, e-mail them to The Wedge Group at: **randy@randyschwantz.com**. We'll edit them and send them back to you ready to go.

Components of The Prospect Interview

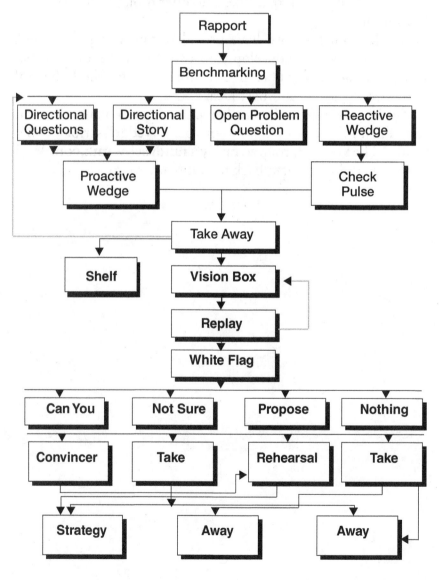

Take Away Lines

TAKE AWAY VERBIAGE:

[ ] Maybe it's not that important BECAUSE:
[ ] I guess it's not that big a deal BECAUSE:
[ ] I could tell you that this is really huge and important and that
     you should really pay attention to it but I know you expect me to
     say that — although it could be the truth — it's just not that
     important BECAUSE:

Claims review	It will never happen again
Safety meetings	You have a screening process that prevents you from hiring anyone who could get hurt
Payroll audit	You could easily pay this out of petty cash
Coverage checklist	If something was not covered your agent would pay for it out of his commissions
Attentiveness, quarterly visits	Your guy doesn't make enough money off your account to justify that type of service
Sales growth	Your personal obligations like buying cars, college educations, and weddings will be handled by someone else
Sales efficiencies	You've got a lot of support staff to pick up the pieces

Reactive Wedge
Who, What, How & Why

When you told **WHO** that you did not like/were not happy with **PROBLEM** and that you wanted them to **WHAT, HOW, and WHY**, What did they say?

MAKES UP
PICTURE PERFECT
↙   ↘

WHO	PROBLEM	WHAT	HOW	WHY
Your agent	Late certificates	Systematic process	Where they requests and send out a fax ASAP so you get it that day	So you don't have to worry about not getting on job sites or getting your invoices paid

Rehearsal Script

Script out your <u>Rehearsal</u> - play off of...

S: Suppose for a moment that it's three weeks from now and you're looking at my proposal. It has all the elements you said you wanted. Can you imagine that?

P: OK, I can imagine that

S: As you look at the proposal you say to yourself, I think we've found a new agent. But that creates a new dilemma and I'm wondering, can we deal with that?

P: What is that?

S: The problem is that when you decide I'm your new guy, how are you going to tell the other guy that it's over?

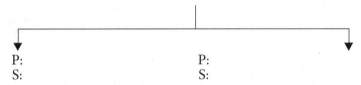

P: P:

S: S:

Convincer Strategy

Script out your <u>Convincer Strategy</u> - play off of...

P: Can you do that?

S: Sure, we can do that, but you expect me to say that don't you? Because you still see me as a salesperson, right?

P: Yes, I do.

S: So, how would you know that what I'm telling you is true...that we can do that? Do have to see letters of reference or an action plan? Do you have to talk to some people and let them tell you we can do it? Or, do you rely on your gut feeling to say, Yes, he's telling me the truth or no, he's lying to me. How would you know that what I'm telling you is true, that we really can do this?

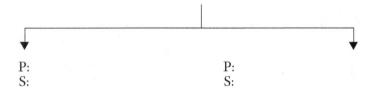

P: P:

S: S:

Best Deal Close Script

Script out your <u>Best Deal Close</u> - play off of...

S: What would have to happen for you to be willing to take my best deal and his best deal and let the best deal win? No second looks, no going back to the underwriter, no midnight negotiations, and no last minute "slam dunks." My best deal and his best deal and let the best deal win. What would have to happen for you to be willing to do that?

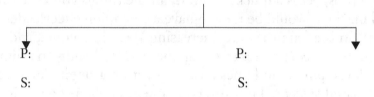

P: P:

S: S:

Sneak Preview: iWin

We've all invested in and used them—commercial, sales management software programs that never quite live up to our expectations. Over the years, they've certainly gotten better, but never quite good enough.

For one thing, they're not specific to the insurance industry. For another, the programs themselves can be cumbersome memory hogs on our personal computers. And who remembers to back-up?

And then there's the real issue that stalls your sales process. Hint: it's not the name of the prospect's youngest child. What you need is an arsenal of Wedges that work. What you need when you're sitting in the parking lot waiting for your face-to-face with a new prospect is a quick review of all the things you've learned. And maybe it would be nice to have a champion cheerleader.

iWin is an approach to Increasing Wealth, Income, and Net Worth that incorporates tracking, forecasting, hands-on training, skill development and sales coaching within a single, integrated, Web-based system. The core component of the program is *The Wedge*, coupled with the best of *Red Hot Introductions*, and *Breaking the Sales Barrier* — the entire Wedge Group repertoire.

Want to know more? Go to https://-iwin2.thewedge.net